John Conroy Hutcherson

Tom Finch's Monkey

John Conroy Hutcherson

Tom Finch's Monkey

ISBN/EAN: 9783743318755

Manufactured in Europe, USA, Canada, Australia, Japa

Cover: Foto ©ninafisch / pixelio.de

Manufactured and distributed by brebook publishing software (www.brebook.com)

John Conroy Hutcherson

Tom Finch's Monkey

Tom Finch's Monkey

And How he Dined with the Admiral

AND OTHER YARNS

BY

JOHN C. HUTCHESON

Author of "The Wreck of the Nancy Bell" "Picked up at Sea" &c.

ILLUSTRATED

BLACKIE AND SON LIMITED
LONDON GLASGOW AND BOMBAY

CONTENTS.

	PAGE

TOM FINCH'S MONKEY,
    AND HOW HE DINED WITH THE ADMIRAL . . 5

THE ESCAPE OF THE "CRANKY JANE.
    A STORY ABOUT AN ICEBERG. 35

THE GREEK BANDIT.
    A REMINISCENCE OF A YACHTING CRUISE IN THE
        ÆGEAN SEA. 75

JIM NEWMAN'S YARN:
    OR, A SIGHT OF THE SEA SERPENT. . . 103

"OUR SCRATCH ELEVEN."
    A TALE OF A CRICKET MATCH . . . 131

TOM FINCH'S MONKEY;

AND HOW HE DINED WITH THE ADMIRAL.

WE were cruising off Callao on the Pacific station when it all happened, and I daresay there are a good many others who will recollect all about it as well as myself. But to explain the matter properly I must go back a little in my dates; for, instead of Callao at the commencement of my yarn, you must read Calabar.

You see, I was in the *Porpoise* at the time, a small old-fashioned, paddle-wheel steamer that had been ordered across from the West Coast of Africa by "my lords" of the Admiralty to reinforce our squadron in South American waters on account of a war breaking out between Chili and Peru. Being a "sub" on board of her, and consequently subject to the authorities that be, when the *Porpoise* was obliged to abandon the fragrant mangrove swamps at the mouth of the Congo river, where we had been enjoying ourselves for over a twelvemonth amidst the delights of a deadly miasma that brought on perpetual low fever, and as constant a consumption of quinine and bottled beer to counteract its effects, I was of course forced to accompany her across the Atlantic and round the Horn to her allotted destination.

Thence "this plain unvarnished tale," which is as clear as mud in a ditch, although you needn't believe it if you don't like—there is no compulsion required to make hungry people eat roast mutton!

Tom Finch, the lieutenant in command of the *Porpoise*, who had got his promotion through the death vacancy of his senior at Cape Coast Castle—he was just ahead of me on the roster, luckily for him—was one of the jolliest fellows I ever sailed with or under, since I entered the service; and I'm sure I've known a few "swabs" in my time!

Unlike some junior officers I could name, when suddenly intrusted with the reins of power, there was nothing of the martinet about Tom, even on the first day he assumed his new rank, when a little extra pomposity might have been excusable. But no, he gave himself no airs or graces whatever.

He was the same Tom Finch who had chaffed and larked and talked confidence with me in the gun-room, now that he trod the quarter-deck "in all his war paint," as I told him somewhat impudently, the "skipper" of H.M.S. *Porpoise*, "paddle sloop, 6 guns," as she was described in the *Navy List*—the same unaffected, jovial, good-natured sailor whom everybody liked, men and messmates alike. His only weakness was a love for practical joking, which he would carry out sometimes, perhaps, to a rather ticklish extent—for his own good, that is, as he never knowingly did anyone else an injury by it.

"What will you do with your monkey?' I said, when the mail brought in our orders from the commodore on the West Coast for us to sail for Monte Video at once, and there await our further instructions—which would be sent on from England; "what will you do with him when we go?"

"Take him with me of course," answered Tom; "why shouldn't I?"

"Well, I don't see any reason against it certainly," I replied; "now that you are captain of the ship, and can do as you please without asking anybody's leave."

"Poor Griffin," said Tom, "he *did* object to Jocko's society; that was the reason I always used to keep the dear fellow ashore; however, as you say, Gerald, I am my own master and can do as I like now. You don't think the crew dislike my monkey, do you?" he added eagerly.

He was such a kind-hearted obliging chap, that if he thought that even the loblolly boy objected to the presence of Jocko on board, he would have banished him from the ship for ever, especially from the very fact of his being the commander and having no one to dispute his authority.

"Oh dear, no, certainly not," I replied at once, with "effusion," as the French say in their idiom. "The men like him better than you do, if that is possible; and I don't know what they would do without him, I only thought the change of climate might be deleterious to his health, that's all!"

"Deleterious indeed, Gerald! wherever did you pick up such a fine word? I suppose you have been interviewing old Jalap about your liver, eh, you hypochondriacal young donkey! Why, Monte Video is a regular paradise for the monkey tribe, and Jocko will be in his element there!"

"But I don't suppose we'll stop there, Tom; didn't you say that you thought it probable that we would have to go round Cape Horn and join the squadron at Callao?"

I may here explain that while on the quarter-deck, I invariably addressed Tom Finch as "Sir," for was he not my commanding officer? But, while below, or when off duty, he insisted on my retaining my old custom of calling him by his Christian name, the same as when we were together in the gun-room, and he only a "sub."

"And if we *do* go round the Horn, what then, Mr. Sub-lieutenant Follett?" said he.

"Won't Jocko find it cold: you know it's winter time there now?"

"And can't I have him clothed like a Christian, stupid, and keep him by the fire, or in the cook's cabin, where he will be so warm, that he'll fancy himself in his native clime?"

"Oh, yes," said I, "I quite forgot that his dearest friend next to you was Pompey!" alluding to the ship's cook, a sable African, who came very probably from the same locality as the monkey; the two being very much alike, not only in the colour of their complexions, but in their features and facial development.

"Yes," said Tom reflectively, "Pompey will take care he doesn't freeze. He could not be fonder of him than his own brother would be; he might, indeed, *be* his relative, if Darwin's theory should prove to be true! However, I must see about getting Jocko rigged out properly in a decent sailor's suit so that he may get accustomed to the clothing before we come to the cold latitudes. I daresay my marine, who is a smart fellow, can manage to cut down a guernsey frock and a pair of canvas or serge trousers to fit the brute: I will give an order on the paymaster for them at once and Smith can set to work on them without delay;" and he bustled out of his cabin to carry his intentions into effect.

Not being intimately acquainted with even the rudimentary elements of natural history, I cannot say to what order or genus of the monkey family Jocko belonged; but, roughly speaking, I think he was a specimen of chimpanzee or small gorilla, as he had no tail, and when he walked erect, which was his favourite position, he looked uncommonly like the "superior animal."

Tom Finch had shot the monkey's mother in the bush when on a hunting excursion up the interior of the country, which he indulged in on first coming to the coast; and having captured and nursed the youngster with the utmost solicitude, Jocko repaid his master's attention by learning so many tricks and imitating the deportment of those with whom he was brought in contact so carefully, that he was now, at the time of which I speak, such a thoroughly educated and well-bred monkey as to be "um purfit genelman," as Pompey, the cook, said—one "fit to shine in any circle," especially on ship-board, where he was an endless source of amusement to us all, from the lieutenant-commander down to the loblolly boy aforesaid.

Pursuant to Tom Finch's directions and the exertions of his marine servant Smith, before we left the mouth of the Congo our friend Jocko was decorously habited in a smart seafaring costume; and, long ere we had crossed the Atlantic and arrived at Monte Video, the intelligent animal had got so habituated to his new rig that the difficulty would have been to persuade him to go about once more in his former unclothed state—and yet some sceptics say that monkeys aren't human! You should only have seen him walking up and down the quarter-deck, or on the bridge by Tom's side, he looked for all the world like a juvenile "reefer!"

It was in the cabin, however, that Jocko's acquirements came out in the strongest relief. Tom had taught him to sit at table and use a spoon or fork in helping himself from his plate as naturally as possible; and, as for drinking, you should only have seen him pour out a tumbler of bottled stout, for which he had an inordinate relish, and tossing it down his throat, give a sigh of the deepest satisfaction when he had finished it, when, replacing his glass on the table, he would lean back in his chair as if overcome by the exertion.

Before he had been clothed in sailor fashion, Jocko used to be very fond of skylarking with the men forward, stealing their mess utensils and scampering up and down the rigging to evade pursuit when his mischievousness had been found out; but, after that period, he seemed to become possessed of a wonderful amount of dignity which made him give up his wild frolicsomeness, and leave off his previous habits, for he never went to the forecastle again, but restricted himself to the officers' quarters aft. This he did, too, in spite of the coaxings of the crew, who were very fond of him, and the fact of Tom often kicking him out of his cabin, where he would take possession of his sofa whenever he had the chance, wrapping himself in Tom's boat cloak and reclining gracefully on the cushions. One of Jocko's chief amusements also was in watching the machinery when in motion; and he would spend hours in looking down at it through the engine-room hatch.

Once, when the skylight was up, he had a narrow squeak for his life; for, carried away by his excitement, in trying to put his hands—paws I should say—on the revolving shaft, he tumbled through; and, but for the chief engineer seeing him in time and stopping the engines, which were just then going slow, poor Jocko would have come to grief.

This accident, however, never broke him of the habit of inspecting the machinery. It had a sort of weird attraction for him which he could not resist. Possibly, he might have been a sort of incubating Watt or Brunel, who knows? But, alas, he never became sufficiently developed or "evolved" from his quadrumanous condition to answer the question in person, as the engines which were his hobby in the end compassed his untimely death!

Those paddle-wheel steamers that were built for the navy some forty years ago, although designed for capturing Cuban slavers, were certainly not remarkable for their speed, and the *Porpoise* was no exception to her class; so, what with her naturally slow rate of progression through the water, and the strict Admiralty circular limiting the consumption of coal even on special service like ours, we did not make a very rapid passage across the south Atlantic to Monte Video. This place is charmingly situated on the estuary of the Rio de la Plata, and very appropriately named; for it can be seen far away off, for miles at sea, and itself commands magnificent views of its own beautiful harbour and the surrounding inland scenery.

Here despatches awaited us, as Tom Finch had previously been informed at Cape Coast Castle would be the case, ordering the *Porpoise* to proceed immediately to the Pacific and join the admiral on that station at Callao; and, accordingly, after one of the briefest of stays at a port which I have always longed since to have a more extended acquaintanceship with, we up anchor and paddled away to our assigned rendezvous— not by way of the "Horn," which we did not go round, as I had imagined we would, for it was far too stormy; but, through the Straits of Magellan, which are easy enough of passage to a steamer, independent almost of winds and currents, although somewhat perilous to sailing vessels, especially during the winter months.

Jocko seemed to feel the cold as soon as we began to run down towards Terra del Fuego, and had some additional garments placed round him; but true to what he evidently thought was his new and proper position, he would not take up his quarters with his "old friend and brother," Pompey, in the cook's caboose, preferring to shiver in Tom's cabin till he almost turned blue.

"Bress dat Massa Jocko!" Pompey would say after a vain attempt to coax him to share his hospitality. "I can't make he out nohow! Guess he tinks himself buckra ossifer and bery fine genelman, now de captin take um into cabin, sure; but, he no rale genelman to turn up nose at um ole frens! No, sah, I no spik to him no more!" and the negro cook would retire with ill-suppressed anger, which was all the more amusing to us from its having been occasioned by a monkey!

On our getting round into the Pacific, and

sighting the coast towards Valparaiso, where we had to stop and coal once more, the *Porpoise* not having much storage room in her old bunkers, Jocko got more on friendly terms with the thermometer, making faces and jabbering away in his lingo, which unfortunately no one but himself could understand, just as if he were still in his native clime on the African continent.

Occasionally, too, as if his spirits carried him away on his restoration to warmer latitudes, he would indulge in one of his old skylarking bouts with the crew, and even made advances to Pompey in his caboose, which that worthy, in spite of his indignation at the manner in which he had been treated by Jocko when he assumed the dignity of the *toga virilis*, was only too glad to welcome and reciprocate; but, after one of these unusual unbendings, the monkey grew even more dignified and inapproachable than before, except to Tom and myself, who could do anything with him, and he then confined himself exclusively to the cabin and quarter-deck.

At Valparaiso we got further despatches hurrying us up to the Peruvian coast, where the admiral much wanted to use us as a despatch vessel; so, taking in as much coal as our old tub, the *Porpoise*, could cram into her, we started for Callao, steaming hard day and night all this time—but it took us no less than ten days to reach our port at last.

The admiral's ship was in the offing as we entered the harbour; and, without the slightest warning or time for preparation after we had made our muster, the old gentleman signalled, much to Tom's discomposure, that he was coming on board of us for inspection at once.

"A pretty kettle of fish!" exclaimed Tom; "just as if he couldn't give a fellow time to paint up a bit and look tidy after sweltering all the pitch off her for eighteen months on the coast, and scuttling across the Atlantic as if the deuce were after us, and not a day allowed us to overhaul and make the old ship look presentable—why, it's too bad!"

"You needn't grumble, sir," said I—we were both on the quarter-deck now, and the *friend* had, of course, to yield to the *officer* —"I'm sure the admiral won't be able to find much fault with the *Porpoise*, even if he were predetermined to do so, as she's in apple-pie order!"

And so she was; while her crew, who almost worshipped Tom and would have followed him to a man anywhere, were in the highest state of discipline and health, the African fever having disappeared almost as soon as we lost sight of the pestilential West Coast and got into blue water.

"Do you think so, Follett?" he said more calmly.

"Certainly," I answered, "I would back her against any other vessel on the station for being in the highest state of efficiency."

"I'm glad you think so, Gerald," he said to me aside, so that the middies who went to man the side ropes for the admiral at the gangway could not hear him. "You know these big guns are always sharp on a fellow who holds a first command; and, as I have no interest to back me up at the Admiralty board, I don't want a bad report to go in against me, and a black mark be set before my name for ever!"

"Don't you fear, Tom," said I cheerfully, "you'll pass muster with flying colours!"

Well, the admiral came on board and the inspection turned out just as I expected.

Not only was the gallant chief satisfied with the condition of the *Porpoise;* but, after having mustered the men at quarters, and having them exercised at gun-drill and cutlasses, he was so pleased that he publicly complimented Tom Finch on the state of his ship and crew, saying that they were not only creditable to him, but to the service generally.

So far, so good.

When the admiral, however, descended presently to Tom's cabin to sign papers, and perhaps to give a look around him, too, to see how such an efficient officer comported himself when "at home" so to speak, Tom's evil genius placed Master Jocko in the way.

There he was, seated on the sofa, dressed up in some nondescript sort of uniform with which the youngsters had invested him during Tom's absence on deck—the young imps were always up to some of their larks, and being of a kindred disposition himself, Tom was never hard on them for their tricks.

The monkey had on a blue coat and trousers with a red sash across his chest and a Turkish fez on his head, which gave him the appearance of one of the many Chilian field marshals, and generals, and colonels whom we had seen at Valparaiso, his wizened, dried-up face adding to the delusion.

As luck would have it, too, what should Jocko do, as the admiral and Tom entered the cabin, but rise from the sofa; and taking off the cap from his head with one of his paws, while the other was laid deferentially on his chest, he made a most polite bow, in the manner he had always been used to do, when either of us greeted him on coming in.

"Who's this gentleman?" said the admiral pleasantly, taking off *his* cocked hat likewise, and returning the salute—" I suppose someone you've given a passage to on the way, eh?"

Tom was at his wit's end, as he told me afterwards, for the moment; but his native "nous" came to the rescue, and, combined with his love of a practical joke, suggested a loophole of escape.

"Oh, sir," said he, "this is one of the aides-de-camp of the Chilian generalissimo, a Senor Carrambo, who begged me to land him at Callao on some urgent private business. Of course, I know, sir, of the hostilities between his native state and Peru, and that as a neutral I ought not to offer any means of communication between the two powers; but, sir, as you see for yourself, he's a very harmless sort of fellow, and—"

"Hush!" said the admiral, apparently shocked at Tom's speaking out in such an off-hand way his opinion of the foreign gentleman, as he took Jocko to be.

"Oh, bless you," went on Tom, forgetting for the moment to whom he was speaking— "he cannot understand a word of English, and I can't make out a single word of his Chilian Spanish—but he's very polite."

"So I see," replied the admiral affably, as master Jocko made another obeisance at this juncture; "pray ask him to accompany you on board the flagship with me to dinner. Tell him I shall feel honoured by his company, as indeed I shall be by yours."

To say he was thunderstruck at the admiral's request would not convey the slightest idea of Tom's mental condition when he found himself in such a dilemma.

He could have bitten off his tongue for its having got him into such a scrape, by telling the fib about the monkey in the first instance; but it was too late now, for the admiral had turned to leave the cabin, and the marine was at the door, besides others, who would hear any explanation he might make.

Tom determined, therefore, with a courage that was almost heroic, to carry the thing through to the bitter end—giving me a pathetic wink to instruct everybody to "keep the thing dark" on board—for none knew about Jocko excepting our ship's company.

Furtively shoving the fez down over the monkey's head, so that it almost concealed its features, he threw the boat cloak that rested on the sofa around him; and, taking hold of his paw, marched in the admiral's wake to the gangway, and thence down into the chief's barge alongside, where the admiral and he and Jocko took their seats in state in the stern-sheets and were rowed off to the flagship—our crew manning the rigging as they left and giving three hearty cheers!

"I like to see that proof of affection in your men," said the admiral, as he witnessed this unofficial performance. "They are proud of their commander, and, I am sure, you have a crew to be proud of!"

Tom bowed in acknowledgment of the compliment. He knew well enough what had occasioned the enthusiasm of the blue-jackets, and bit his lips to restrain his laughter, which so suffocated him that he felt he would burst if he had to keep it in much longer!

All he could do now was to brazen out the imposture, and he huddled the boat-cloak round Jocko so as to conceal his form.

"Poor Senor Carrambo is suffering fearfully from the ague," he said in explanation to the admiral of this little attention on his part— "I'm afraid he should not have ventured out of the cabin."

"A good glass of sherry will soon warm him," said the admiral smiling, "and I think I shall be able to offer him one."

"He's rather partial to bottled ale or stout," suggested Tom, "and he may possibly prefer that."

"Rather a queer taste for a Spaniard," said the admiral, as the barge reached the side of the flagship; "but I think I can also gratify on board my ship this predilection of Senor —eh?"

"Carrambo," prompted Tom.

"Yes, Carrambo," added the admiral as he mounted the accommodation ladder of the flagship—Tom Finch with Jocko on his arm following in his wake, as before, amidst the mutual salutes of the admiral and the officers, to the state cabin of the chief.

Seated at the dinner-table, to which all were summoned with all proper ceremony to the exhilarating tune of the "Roast beef of old England," Jocko, who had a chair alongside of Tom, behaved with the utmost decorum.

He indeed appeared to eat little but bread, biscuit, tart, and fruit; but, beyond a grimace, which must have caused the admiral to reflect that of all the ugly persons he ever beheld in his life, this Chilian officer was certainly the ugliest, nothing particularly happened, and the dinner passed off without an exposure.

Tom, the admiral observed, frequently helped "the generalissimo's aide-de-camp," especially in pouring out his wine, which he limited in a marked degree; but the jocular lieutenant-commander passed this off by saying that his distinguished friend—whom he exchanged a word with occasionally, of some outlandish language, a mixture of Spanish and High Dutch, with a sprinkling of the Chinese tongue—was in the most feeble health and acting under the docter's directions regarding his diet:—that was the reason also, he explained, of his remaining cloaked and with his head-covering on at the admiral's table, for which he craved a thousand pardons!

After dinner, Tom would have given worlds to have beaten a retreat to his own ship, as several officers came into the saloon while coffee was handed round, and he dreaded each moment that Jocko would disgrace himself and the bubble would burst; but no, there the admiral would keep him, talking all the time, and directing most of his attention towards the pseudo "Senor Carrambo," for whose benefit Tom had to translate, or pretend to translate, what was said.

Tom said he never got so punished for a joke in his life before, and he took very good care not to let his sense of the ridiculous put him in such a plight again, as for more than two mortal hours he suffered all the tortures of a condemned criminal; as he said, he would rather have been shot at once!

But when the admiral shook hands with him on his departure, Tom felt worst of all.

"Good-bye, lieutenant," said the admiral, "and thanks for your introduction to 'Senor Carrambo.' I admired the condition and discipline of your ship to-day, Mr. Finch, and, in forming my opinion of your character I must say that you carry out a joke better than anyone I ever met. *But you should remember, lieutenant, that those who have the end of the laugh, enjoy the joke best.* Good-night, I shall communicate with you to-morrow!"

Poor Tom! after believing that the admiral had suspected nothing up to the last moment, to be thus undeceived.

It was heartrending!

Gone was his commission, he thought, at one fell blow, with all the pleasant dreams of promotion that had flashed across his brain after the admiral's encomiums on him that afternoon; and he would have to think himself very lucky if he were not tried by court-martial and dismissed the service with disgrace.

It was paying dearly for a practical joke, played off on the spur of the moment, truly!

When he reached the *Porpoise* he felt so disgusted that he kicked poor Jocko, boat-cloak, fez and all, down the main hatch, gruffly ordered his gig to be triced up to the davits, and went below to brood over his anticipated disgrace in the solitude of his own cabin, where I presently found him.

After a great deal of persuasion, I got him to indite a letter of apology to the admiral, detailing all Jocko's perfections, and how he had been constantly an inmate of his cabin; while assuring him that the passing off the monkey as a "foreigner" had not been a planned thing, but was only the result of an accident and his own unaccountable love of fun, although the falsehood he had been guilty of was most reprehensible.

Indeed, as I made him observe, if it had not been for the admiral himself suggesting the imposture, he, Tom, would never have dreamt of it; but, he concluded, he would regret it all his life, for he had not only told a lie, but the whole matter appeared like a deliberately contemplated insult to his superior officer.

This letter Tom, still acting under my advice, sent off immediately to the flagship, as it was yet not late, and within half an hour he received an answer which made him dance an Indian war-dance of delight around the cabin table, where he and I were awaiting the news that was to make or mar poor Tom's future life.

The admiral's ran thus:—

"Flag, at Sea, July, 18—.

Dear Commander,
    I accept your apology, and forgive the joke which I enjoyed, I believe, more than you did, having discovered Master Jocko's identity from the first moment when he took his Turkish fez off to salute me in the cabin, on my entering—you young rascal! I would not have missed for a hundred pounds the agony you were in all the time you were sitting at my table, and, I really think, I had the best of the joke!

Come and breakfast with me and I will tell you the reason *why I address you as above*—I suppose he never told you, but your father was one of my dearest friends.

Yours, with best compliments to 'Senor Carrambo,'

Anson."

"By George, Tom," said I when we had both perused this letter, "you are in luck! He doesn't call you *Commander* for nothing!"

"No, I suppose not," said he, "at all events, Gerald, he's a trump! I recollect my old father saying something once about asking him to put in a good word for me; but, I daresay he forgot all about it: but I am none the worse for it now, eh?"

"No," said I, "thanks to Jocko!"

The next day Tom Finch had his commission made out by the admiral's secretary as commander of the *Blanche*, while I was promoted to his place in the *Porpoise*, owing to the good word he put in for me when he breakfasted with the jolly old chief; and we both of us were busy enough the next few months on the station, protecting British interests and stopping would-be privateers from having such a festive time as they expected during the period that hostilities lasted between the two rival South American republics at the time of which I speak; then wars between Chili and Peru, and the rest of these very independent states, being of as periodic occurrence as the yellow fever in the Gulf of Mexico!

Poor Jocko, as I hinted at before, came finally to grief in a very sad way.

We were chasing a suspicious looking blockade-runner, a short time after he had his remarkable invitation to dine with the admiral; our engines were moving a little more rapidly than usual; and, Jocko, who was perched on the skylight above, was looking at them with the most intense interest.

All at once, the platform on which he was resting slipped, and the talented monkey fell into the engine-room, in the midst of the machinery—there was one sharp agonized squeak, and the last page of poor Jocko's history was marked with the word *Finis!*

THE
ESCAPE OF THE "CRANKY JANE."

THE ESCAPE OF THE "CRANKY JANE."

A STORY ABOUT AN ICEBERG.

ONE day, some three years ago or so, I chanced to be down at Sheerness dockyard; and, while there, utilized my time by inspecting the various vessels scattered about this naval repository. Some of the specimens exhibited all the latest "improvements" in marine architecture, being built to develop every destructive property—huge floating citadels and infernal machines; while others were old, and now useless, types of the past "wooden walls of old England," ships that once had braved the perils of the main in all the panoply of their spreading canvas, and whose broadsides had thundered at Trafalgar, making music in the ears of the immortal Nelson and his compeers.

Amongst the different craft that caught my eye—old hulks, placidly resting their weary timbers on the muddy bosom of the Medway, dismantled, dismasted, and having pent-houses like the roofs of barns over their upper decks in lieu of awnings; armour-plated cruisers, in the First Class Steam Reserve, ready to be commissioned at a moment's notice; and ships in various degrees of construction, on the building slips and in dry dock—was a vessel which seemed to be undergoing the operation of "padding her hull," if the phrase be admissible as explaining what I noticed about her, the planking, from which the copper sheathing had been previously stripped, being doubled, apparently, and protected in weak places by additional beams and braces being fixed to the sides. Of course, I may be all wrong in this, but it was what seemed to me to be the case.

On inquiry I learnt that the vessel was the *Alert*, which it may be recollected was one of the two ships in the Arctic expedition commanded by Sir George Nares. I wondered why so many workmen were busy about her, hammering, sawing, planing, riveting, fitting and boring holes with giant gimlets, so I asked the reason for this unwonted activity, when it might have been reasonably supposed that the vessel had played her part in the service and might have been allowed to pass the remainder of her days afloat in an honourable retreat up the estuary on which the dockyard stands.

But, no.

I was informed that the *Alert* had yet many more days of Arctic experience in store for her, our government having placed her at the disposal of the United States authorities to take part in the relief of Lieutenant Greeley's Polar expedition.—I may here mention in parenthesis that the vessel subsequently successfully performed the task committed to her substantial frame; and it was mainly by means of the stores deposited by her in a *câche* in Smith Sound that the survivors of the expedition were enabled to be transported home again in safety.—I, really, only mention the vessel's name on account of the man who told me about her—a gentleman who entered into conversation with me about the cold regions of the north generally, and of the escapes of ships from icebergs in particular.

He was a seafaring man. I could see that at a glance, although he was not one I should have thought who had donned her majesty's uniform, for he lacked that dapper look that the blue-jackets of the service are usually distinguished by; but he was a veritable old salt, or "shell-back," none the less, sniffing of the ocean all over, and having his face seamed with those little venous streaks of pink (as if he indulged in a dab of rouge on the sly occasionally) which variegate the tanned countenances of men exposed to all the rigours of the elements, and who encounter with an equal mind the freezing blast of the frozen sea or the blazing sun of Africa.

I told this worthy that once, when on a voyage in one of the Inman line of steamers from Halifax to Liverpool, I had gone—or rather the vessel had, to be more correct—perilously near an iceberg, when my nautical friend proceeded to give vent to his own exposition of the "glacial theory," saying that a lot of nonsense was written about the ice in the Arctic regions by people who never went beyond their own firesides at home and had never seen an iceberg. It made him mad, he said, to read it!

"I daresay you've read a lot of rubbish on the subject?" said the old gentleman, getting excited about the matter, as if he only wanted a good start to be off and away on his hobby.

"I daresay I have," I replied.

"Well, what with all the fiction that has been written and the fabulous stories told of the Arctic and its belongings, the 'green hand' who makes the voyage for the first time is full of expectations concerning all the wonderful sights he's going to see in 'the perennial realms of ice and snow'—that's the phrase the newspaper chaps always use—expectations which are bound to be disappointed, —and why?"

"I'm sure I can't tell," said I.

"Because the things that he fancies he's going to see don't really exist, nor never yet did in spite of what book-learned people may say! The voyager who goes north for the first time is bound, let us say for illustration, for Baffin's Bay; and, from what he has learnt beforehand, bears and walruses, seals and sea-lions, whale blubber and the Esquimaux who eat it, all occupy some considerable share of his imagination. But, above all these, the first thing that he looks forward to see are the icebergs, or floating mountains of ice, which are so especially the creation of the cold regions to which he is sailing. These icebergs, sir, form the staple background of every Arctic view, without which none would be deemed for a moment complete. Their gigantic peaks and jagged precipices are familiar to most, in a score of pictures and engravings drawn by artists who were never beyond the Lizard Lights; and really, I believe that if one was sketched that wasn't at least a thousand feet high or more, and didn't have a polar bear perched on top and a full rigged ship sailing right underneath it, why, the generality of people would think it wasn't a bit like the real thing!"

"And what is the 'real thing' like?" I asked with some curiosity.

"There you have me," said the old sailor, who had from his speech evidently received a good education; and if once "before the mast" had now certainly risen to something much higher. "To men whose minds have been wrought up to such a pitch of fancy and expectation, the first sight of a real iceberg is a complete take-down to their imagination. Your ship is pitching about, say, in the cross seas near the mouth of Davis Strait, preparatory to entering within the smooth water of the Arctic circle, when in the far distance your eye catches sight of a lump of ice, looking, as it rises and falls sluggishly in the trough of the sea, not unlike a hencoop covered with snow, after it had been pitched overboard by some passing ship, or like a gigantic lump of foam tossed on the crest of a wave. If the day is sunless, the reflection of light which gives it that glistening appearance, so remarkable as the midnight sun glances among an array of these objects, is wanting to add dignity to the contour of what it is a rude dissipation of life's young dream to learn is an iceberg—though on a very small scale. It is simply a wave-worn straggler from the fleet which will soon be met sailing southward out of the Greenland fjords. The warm waters of the Atlantic will in the course of a few days be too much for it. The sun will be at work on it; it will get undermined by the wash of the breakers, until, being top-heavy, it will speedily capsize. Then the war between the ice and the elements will begin afresh, until the once stately ice-mountain will become the 'bergy bit,' as whalers call the slowly-lessening mass of crumbling, spongy ice, until it finally disappears in the waters; but only to rise again in the form of vapour, which the cold of the north will convert into snow, the parent of that inland ice about the polar regions which forms the source of subsequent icebergs afresh—the process being always going on, never ending!"

"Why, you are quite a philosopher," I observed.

"A bit of a one, sir," said the old gentleman with a smile. "Those who go down to the sea in ships, you know, see wonders in the deep! But, to continue what I was telling you about the icebergs. As your ship proceeds further north they become more numerous and of larger dimensions, until, as you pass the entrance of some of those great fjords, or inlets, which intersect the Greenland coast-line, they pour out in such numbers that the wary mariner is thankful for the continuous daylight and summer seas that enable him so easily to avoid these floating rocks. Here are several broken-up ones floating about in the Waigat, a narrow strait between the island of Disco and the mainland of Greenland, and in close vicinity to several fjords noted for sending big bergs adrift in the channel way to float southward. These are the 'ice mountains' of the fancy artist. One ashore close into the land, and yet not stranded or on account of its depth in the water getting into any very shallow soundings, you may see in your mind's eye, as I've seen them scores of times in reality. It presents to your notice a dull white mass of untransparent ice—not transparent, with objects to be seen through it on the other side, as I have noticed in more than one picture of the North Pole taken by an artist on the spot! This mass is generally jagged at the top with saw-like edges, and it doesn't so very much resemble those Gothic cathedral spires as Arctic writers try to make out. Still, on the whole, the shape of this monster floating mass of ice is very striking to those seeing it for the first time; and when you come to look at it more closely, its size and general character lose nothing by having the details ciphered down, as a Yankee skipper would say."

"Are the icebergs very big?" I inquired.

"Well," said the old gentleman, quite pleased at being asked for information on the subject, and evidently wishing to convert me to his own practical way of thinking in opposition to Arctic fiction-mongers, "they may sometimes be seen of a hundred and fifty feet high, occasionally reaching to a couple of hundred, while sometimes I've seen an iceberg that towered up more than double that height; but the majority of them do not exceed a hundred feet at most. The colour, as I've said, is not emerald green, as most folks think—that is, not unless it is seen under what science-folks call the prismatic action of light—but a dull white that is almost opaque. The sides are, generally, dripping with the little streams of water formed by the melting of the ice, and glistening in the rays of the sun; but a dull white is the principal colour of the mass. Its base is broader than its summit, and is here and there hollowed into little caverns by the action of the waves. The pinnacles seen in the pictures of the illustrated papers I've spoken of are not very plain. Indeed, both the one we are supposing and the other bergs, that are always, like the 'birds of a feather' of the proverb, to be seen close together, are flattened on the top; and if here and there worn into fantastic shapes by the weather, they mostly go back to a shape which may be roughly described as broader at the base than the top; otherwise the berg would speedily capsize. When this happens, they go over with a tremendous splash, rocking and churning up the sea for miles round, and sending wave circles spreading and widening out as from the whirlpool in the centre, in the same way as when a child pitches a stone into a pond.

"On some of the bergs are masses of earth, gravel and stone, proving that they must lately have been connected with the land; for owing to the old bergs becoming undermined by the waves, they soon turn over, and so of course send *their* load to the bottom. An examination of the sides of the ice-mass also shows to the eye some other peculiarities. The greater part of the ice is white and thoroughly full of air-bubbles, which lie in very thin lines parallel to each other; but throughout the white ice there are numerous slight cracks or streaks, of an intensely blue and transparent ice, which, on being exposed to heat, before melting, I've been told by the surgeon of the ship I was in, dissolve into large angular grains. These blue cracks cross and cross over again in the mass of the berg, and may possibly be water which has melted and been frozen again either on the surface of the berg, or in its crevasses or cracks when it was a part of the glacier from which it first came. But, besides the blue ice, in some icebergs may be seen a kind of conglomerate of ice-blocks of various sizes, the spaces between them being filled up with snow or crumbled ice. This conglomerate exists usually in cracks, though it is found also in layers, and even forms large masses of the larger bergs, mixed up with stones and earthy lumps."

"Did you ever have any adventure amongst the icebergs?" I asked the old gentleman at this juncture, thinking I had quite enough of the scientific aspect of the subject, and dreading lest he might dive further into the original composition of ice.

"Not in the Arctic Ocean," he replied; "but once, when I was only a common sailor before the mast and aboard a vessel in the Australian trade, I came across icebergs in the southern latitudes which were mighty perilous; and one of these bergs was, by the way, bigger than any I ever saw in northern seas."

"Tell me all about it," I said, glad to get him on to a regular sea yarn.

The old gentleman was nothing loth; and I noticed that the moment he began to speak of his old experiences as a merchant seaman, he dropped the somewhat affected phraseology in which he had previously been expounding his theories for my information concerning the polar regions and the formation of icebergs—thenceforth speaking much more naturally in the ordinary vernacular of Jack tars.

"I suppose it's forty years ago, more or less," he began, "since I shipped in the brig *Jane*, John Jiggins master, bound from London to Melbourne with an assorted cargo.

"She was a decent-sized brig enough, and handy to manage when she had plenty of sea-room, and a wind right aft; but on a bowline, or when the wind was on the quarter, and there was a bit of a sea on, she kept such a stiff weather helm, and was such a down-right cranky vessel, never bending down to a breeze or lifting to the swell, that it was no wonder that as soon as the hands got used to her ways, and tumbled to her contrary points—and she was that contrary sometimes as to remind you of a woman's temper on washing days, most ladies then being not particularly pleasant, and feeling more inclined to drive a man mad rather than to coax and wheedle him—as soon as we all got used to her ways, I say, we christened her 'the Cranky Jane;' and that she was more or less, barring when she had a fair wind, with an easy sea and everything agreeable for her, as I said before.

"Old Cap'en Jiggins, however, wasn't of our way of thinking.

"He was the part owner as well as master of the vessel; and loved the old brig—the 'Janey' he called her, the old fool!—like the very apple of his eye, always praising her up to the nines and not allowing anybody to say a word against her sea-going qualities.

"Sometimes, when the man at the wheel would be swearing at the lubberly craft in a silent way, so that you could see he was suffocating himself with passion and ready to burst himself, for the way in which she would fall off, or bowse up into the wind's eye, and try to go her own way, like a horse that gets the bit between his teeth and sets his ears back, then you'd hear old Jiggins a-talking to himself about the blessed old tub.

"'That's it, my beauty! Look how she rides, the darling, like a duck! What a clipper she is, to be sure; so easy to handle! a child could steer her with a piece of thread!'

"When, p'raps it took all one man's strength, and perhaps two, to bring up the beast a single point to the wind!

"In spite of Cap'en Jiggins' praise, I never sailed in such an out and out obstinate craft as that identical *Cranky Jane.* She seemed to have been laid down on the lines and constructed, plank by plank, especially to spile a man's temper! Somehow or other, with the very lightest of breezes—except, as I've said before, we had the wind right dead aft—we could never get her to lay to her course and keep it. She was always falling off and breaking away in every way but the right one, and wanting to go just in the very opposite direction to what we did; exactly like Paddy's pig when he's taking it to market, and he has to whisper in its ear that he's going to Cork, when he really wants to meet the dealer at Bandon!

"This peculiarity of the brig, of course, very

naturally set the men against her; as, although what is usually called a 'dry ship'—that is, the hands could sleep comfortably in the forecastle, instead of being drenched through day and night, by the seas she took in over the bows, as is the case in some clippers I've sailed in—she was so dreadfully hard to steer that a man's trick at the wheel was like going on the treadmill! And yet, that very peculiarity and contrariness that made us cuss and swear too, only induced Captain Jiggins to say occasionally when she was most outrageous wide in her yawing, 'Pretty dear!' or some such trash—this very peculiarity, I say, saved all our lives from the most dreadful fate, and brought us home safe to England after encountering one of the most deadly perils of the deep. Curious, isn't it? But I'll tell you all about it. Here goes for the yarn.

"We had done the voyage out in pretty fair time from London to Port Philip; for, most of the way, the wind was fair and almost dead aft from the meridian of the Cape of Good Hope, down in the 'roaring forties,' till we got to the Heads. Consequently, the brig couldn't help herself but go straight onward, when the trades were shoving her along and while nobody wanted her to tack, or beat up, or otherwise perform any of those delicate little points of seamanship which a true sailor likes to see his ship go through, almost against his own interest, sometimes, as far as hard work is concerned in reefing and furling and taking in sail, or piling on the canvas and 'letting her rip.' So long as nothing of this sort was wanted from her the brig was as easy-going as you could wish and all probably that Cap'en Jiggins thought her; but, you had only just to try to get her to sail up in the wind's eye or run with the breeze a bit ahead of the beam, and you'd soon have seen for yourself how cantankerous she could be!

"No, it was all plain sailing to Port Philip Heads; and even after we had unloaded our home cargo, and went round, first to Sydney, and afterwards to the Fiji Islands—I shan't forget Suva Suva Bay in a hurry, I can tell you. So far, everything went serene; for, no matter where we wanted to go—and you see, the skipper wasn't tied to any especial port to seek a cargo, but being part owner, could please himself by going to the best market; which, being a shrewd man, with his head screwed on straight, you can bet he did!—no matter where we wanted to go, as I say, the wind seemed to favour us, for it was always right astern, and everything set below and aloft, and the wind blowing us there beautifully right before it all the way —just as the old *Jane* liked it, sweet and not too strong!

"So far, going out to Australia, and looking in at Sydney and Fiji and the islands for cargo, and loading up choke-full with just everything that our skipper counted at the highest freight, with no dead weight to break the brig's back—so far, everything went 'highfalutin'' as the Yanks say; but when we came to leave Polynesia—it ought to be christened Magnesia, I consider, for it contains a bigger continent, with a larger number of islands than Europe—and shape a course homewards to the white cliffs of Old Albion, that we longed to see again after our long absence, for we were away good two years in all, the cap'en thinking nothing of time, being his own charterer, so long as he got a good cargo from port to port, and we were engaged on a trading voyage, and not merely out and home again directly—then it was that the *Cranky Jane* came out in her true colours, and made us love her—oh yes! just as the skipper did—over the left!

"Why, sir, she was that aggravating, that, as Bill the boatswain and I agreed, we should have liked to run her ashore on the very first land we came to, beach her and chop her up there and then for firewood; and we wouldn't have been content till we had burned up the very last fragment of her obstinate old hull!

"After leaving Suva Suva Bay, Fiji, where we filled up the last remaining space in the *Cranky Jane's* hold with copra—which is a lot of cocoa-nuts smashed up so as to stow easy, out of which they make oil at home for moderator lamps—we went south further than I ever went before in any ship. Captain Jiggins, as I heard him explaining to the first officer when I was taking my trick at the wheel, and blessing the brig as usual for her stiff helm, intended making the quickest passage that ever was made, he said, by striking down into them outlandish latitudes before he steered east and made the Horn; and I suppose he knew what he was about, as he was as good a navigator as ever handled a sextant. *He* called it great circle sailing; but *I* called it queer-sailing; and so did most of the hands, barring Bill the boatswain, who said the captain was right; but anyways, right or wrong, it led us into an ugly corner, as you shall hear.

"Well, we went down the latitudes like one o'clock, the brig, running free before the north-east monsoon as if she were sailing for a wager in a barge-race on the Thames; and the weather as fine as you please, warm and sunny—too much so, sometimes—so that a man hadn't to do a stroke of work on board, save to take his turn at the wheel. Watch on deck, and watch below, we had nothing to do but loll about, with a stray pull at a brace here and a sheet there, or else walk into our grub and then turn into our bunks; for Cap'en Jiggins was the proper sort of skipper. None of your making work for him when there was nothing to do; but when the hands were wanted, why he did expect them to look alive, and have no skulking—small blame to him, say I, for one!

"We had run down below the parallel of Cape Horn, pretty considerable I should think, when we at last had to ask the old brig to bear up eastwards to lie her proper course; and then you should have seen the tricks she played—confound her! Why, we had to treat her as gingerly as if she were a yacht rounding a mark-boat to make her bear up a point or go to the wind; although I'll give her the credit of saying, if she were cranky—and she was that, and no mistake—she made no leeway, which was a blessing at all events.

"It was some days after we had altered our course to E.S.E., with as much more easterly as we could get out of her—and that wasn't much, try all we could, with as much fore and aft sail as we could get on her—when the weather began to change, and the wind, which had been steadily blowing from the north-east, chopped round a bit more ahead, the sea getting up, and a stray squall coming now and again, which made us more alert trimming the sails, and taking in and letting out canvas as occasion arose. It was no use, however, trying to drive the brig to the eastward any longer with this wind shifting about, humour her as we might; so the skipper altered her course again more to the south, although we were then as far down as we ought to have gone.

"'The darling,' says he to the first officer when he gave the order to lay her head S.S.E., 'she's a little playful with the heavy cargo we've got on board, and wants to keep warm as long as she can! Let her run a hundred miles or so more south, and then we'll fetch up to the Horn, and be able to spin along like winking, just as the beautiful creature wants!'

"Well! it did make us mad to hear the old man talk like this about the clumsy old tub; but of course we couldn't help ourselves, so we only grinned, and said to each other,—

"'Catch us coming again in the *Cranky Jane* when once we're safe ashore!'

"Would you believe it? The blessed brig, although the new course she was on brought the wind aft instead of on her beam, she was that spiteful over it, that, as it was blowing much stronger than it had been, it took two of us to keep her head from deviating from her proper track, and we had hard work to prevent her from breaking off more than she did.

"The wind came on towards the afternoon to blow harder and harder; and by nightfall —you know it gets dark as soon as the sun goes down in those latitudes—we had to shorten sail so much that the *Cranky Jane* was staggering along at the rate of nearly fourteen knots an hour with reefed top-sails and jib and main-sail besides the stay-sails.

"The weather got wilder and wilder as time went on, the heavens quite dark overhead, except an occasional glint of a star which didn't know whether he ought to show or not; but still, although we were pretty far below the equator, the night was warm and even sultry, so that we expected a hurricane, or cyclone, or something of that sort, for it was quite unnatural to feel as if in the tropics when fifty degrees south!

"The cap'en, I know, thought it would

blow by and by, for before he turned in he caused even the reefed top-sails and stay-sails to be taken in, and left her snug for the night, with only a close-reefed main-sail and the jib on her.

"'Keep a good look-out, Mr. Stanchion,' says he to the chief officer, as he went down the companion-ladder to his cabin, 'and call me if there's the slightest change.'

"'Ay, ay, sir,' says Mr. Stanchion; and so the skipper goes below with a cheerful goodnight, in spite of the weather looking dirty and squalls being handy before morning.

"Now, as luck would have it—as some folks say, although others put it down to something more than luck—Mr. Stanchion wasn't like one of those jolly, devil-may-care, slap-dash sort of officers, that your regular shell-backs like best. He was a silent, quiet, reflective man, who looked and spoke as if butter wouldn't melt in his mouth; and yet he thought deeper and further than your dash-and-go gentlemen, who act on the spur of the moment without cogitating.

"As soon as the skipper had turned in, he did a thing which perhaps not one officer in a hundred would have done in his place, considering we were on the open ocean out of the track of passing vessels, and that it wasn't much darker than it is on most nights when there's no moon, and the sky is cloudy.

"What do you think it was? Why, he put a man on the look-out on the forecastle, just as if we were going up channel, or in a crowded sea-way! The skipper had meant him to look-out himself, but another wouldn't be amiss, he said.

"Providentally, too, the very man whom he accidentally selected was the very best person he could have placed as look-out, if he had picked the whole crew over from the captain downward; although the mate did not know this when he sang out to him to go on the forecastle.

"This was Pat O'Brien—'Paddy,' as all the hands called him—an Irishman, of course, as you would judge from his name, who had been in one of the Arctic expeditions, which we were speaking of just now. He went out with Sir Leopold M'Clintock I think; but all I know is, that he once was up a whole winter in the Polar Sea, and there had got laid on his back with scurvy, besides having his toes frost-bitten, as he frequently told us when yarning amongst the crew of an evening.

"Generally speaking, he was a careless, happy-go-lucky fellow, and one might have wondered that Mr. Stanchion called him from out the watch that had just came on deck; but, as I said before, the mate could not possibly have made a better selection, as it turned out afterwards.

"Pat O'Brien was a comic chap, full of fun, and always making jokes; so that as soon as he opened his mouth almost to say anything the other fellows would laugh, for they knew that some lark was coming.

"'Be jabers,' says Pat, as he goes forward in obedience to the chief officer's order, 'it's a nice pleasant look-out I'll have all by meeself! while you're coilin' the ropes here, I'll be thinkin' of my colleen there!' and he went out on the fok'sel.

"By and by we could hear him muttering to himself. 'Wurrah, wurrah! Holy mother, can't you let me be aisy!' he sang out presently aloud as if he was suffering from something, or in pain.

"'Look out, ahoy!' hails Mr. Stanchion from aft; 'what's the matter ahead—what are you making all that row about?'

"'Sure an' it's my poor feet, save yer honour, that are hurting of me; they feels the frost terrible!'

"The first mate naturally thought Master Paddy was trying to play off one of his capers on him—for it wouldn't be the first time he tried the game on; so this answer got up his temper, making him shout back an answer to the Irishman that would tell him he wasn't going to catch him napping.

"'Nonsense, man,' he calls out—'frost? Why, you are dreaming! The thermometer is up to over sixty degrees, and it's warm enough almost for the tropics.'

"The hands, of course, thought too that Pat was only joking in his usual way and endeavouring to make fun of Mr. Stanchion; and they waited to hear what would come next from the Irishman, knowing that he was not easily shut up when once he had made up his mind for anything. However, they soon could tell from the tone of voice in which Pat spoke again that he wasn't joking this time, or else he was acting very well in carrying out his joke on the mate; for as we were laughing about his 'poor feet,' which was a slang term in those days, Paddy calls out again in reply to the mate,

"'Faix,' says he, 'it's ne'er a lie I'm telling, yer honour. Be jabers! my feet feel as if they were in the ice now, and frost-bitten all over!'

"Another officer in Mr. Stanchion's place would, as likely as not, have consigned poor Pat to a warmer locality in order to warm his limbs there; but Mr. Stanchion, as I've said, was a man of a different stamp, and a reflective one, too; and the words of the Irishman made him think of something he had read once of a frost-bitten limb having been discovered by a well-known meteorologist to be an unfailing weather-token of the approach of cold. Instead, therefore, of angrily telling Pat to hold his tongue and look out as he ought, Mr. Stanchion went forward and joined him; we on deck, of course, being on the look-out at once.

"Presently, we could see the chief officer and the Irishman on the forecastle, peering out together over the ship's bows as if looking for something.

"'I'm certain, sir,' I heard Pat say earnestly, 'we're near ice whenever my feet feels the cold, yer honour; and there, be jabers, there's the ice-blink, as they calls it in the Arctic seas, and we're amongst the icebergs, as sure as you live!'

"At the same moment, the atmosphere lightened up with a whitish blue light—somewhat like pale moonshine—and Mr. Stanchion shouted out at the top of his voice, louder than we ever dreamt he could speak—

"'Hard a-starboard! Down with the helm for your life!'

"Bill, the boatswain, and I, who were together at the wheel, jammed down the spokes with all our strength; but the blessed brig wouldn't come up to the wind as we wanted her. She wouldn't, although we both almost hung on the wheel and wrenched it off the deck. 'Hard up with the helm, men, do you hear?' again sings out the chief officer, rushing aft as he spoke. 'Hard up, men! all our lives are at stake!'

"And the brig wouldn't come up, try all we could. Bill and I could have screamed with rage; but in another minute we were laughing with joy.

"The light got clear; and there, to our horror, just where we wanted the dear old brig to go—and she wouldn't go, like a sensible creature, although we cursed her for not obeying the helm—was an enormous iceberg rising out of the depths of the ocean, and towering above the masts of the poor *Jane*, which I feel loth to call 'cranky' any longer—as high almost as the eyes could see, like the cliffs at Dover, only a hundred yards higher, without exaggeration! If the brig had come up to the wind, as Mr. Stanchion sang out for us to make her, why, two minutes after, she would have struck full into the iceberg, and running, as she was, good fourteen knots and more under her jib and main-sail, her bows would have stoved in, and we'd all have been in Davy Jones's locker before we could have said Jack Robinson!

"As it was, we weren't out of danger by any means. There were icebergs to the right of us; icebergs astern of us, by which we had passed probably when Pat first complained of feeling the cold; icebergs ahead of us, through which we would have gingerly to make our way, for we had no option with the gale that was blowing but to keep the same course we were on, as to lie to amidst all that ice would be more dangerous even than moving on; and the big, enormous berg we had just escaped was on our left, or port side properly speaking—looking, for all the world, like a curving range of cliffs on some rock-bound coast, as it spread out more than five or six miles in length. It was certainly the biggest iceberg I ever saw in my life, beating to nothing all that I afterwards noticed in the Arctic seas when I went north in the *Polaris;* and perhaps that is the reason why all the ice mounds I saw there became so dwarfed by comparison that they looked quite insignificant.

"Pat kept on the forecastle, looking out and directing the course of the vessel, as the cap'en, who had just come on deck, roused by the noise, thought the Irishman's experience in the Arctic seas would make him more useful even than himself in coursing the ship.

"The skipper was right as usual; and Pat had soon a chance of showing that his choice had not been misplaced.

"'Kape her away! kape her away!' Pat shouted out in a minute or two after the cap'en had come on deck. 'The top of the berg is loosenin', yer honour; and sure it's falling on us it will be in a brace of shakes! Kape her away, or, be jabers, it's lost we'll be for sartin!'

"The old brig, although she wouldn't come up to the wind when we wanted her, and thus saved our lives by disobeying orders, now answered her helm promptly without any demur, and dashed away from the mass of ice before the gale at, I should be ashamed to say what speed.

"Bless the old *Cranky Jane!* How could we ever have reviled her and despised her? She seemed almost as if she had human intelligence and a kind of foresight.

"We only just weathered the berg when

the summit toppled over with a crash, missing the after-part of the brig by a very few yards, and churning up the sea far around with a sort of creamy surf, that dashed over our decks, and swept us fore and aft.

"It was a marvellous escape, and only second to that we had just before had in avoiding running on to the same gigantic mass of floating ice, which had probably come up from the Antarctic regions for the summer season—at least, that was Pat O'Brien's explanation for our meeting with it there.

"All that night and next morning we were passing through bergs of every size, big and little, although none were so large as the one which had been so risky to us—bergs that in their splendid architecture and magnificence, with fantastic peaks and fine pinnacles, that glittered in the rising sun with all the colours of the rainbow, flashing out rays and lights of violet and purple, topaz blue and emerald green, blush rose and pink and red, mingled with shades of crimson and gleams of gold, with a frosting over all of silver and bright white light.—Those who haven't seen an iceberg at sea at sunrise have no idea of the depth and breadth of beauty in nature, though I, one who has served his time before the mast, says so. But, avast with such flummery and wordage!"

"Good gracious me!" I exclaimed, aghast at the old gentleman turning round so completely from the statement he had made when we first entered into conversation. "I thought you said just now that all icebergs were a dull white without any other colour, save a streak of blue sometimes running through them like a vein; and yet, here you are painting them in all the varied tints of the rainbow!"

He was not a bit put out, however, by this accusation of inconsistency.

"This was how they looked at sunrise, which, like a brilliant sunset, as you know, makes a very great difference in the appearance of objects, causing even the most common things to look brilliant, and dignifying the common so as to make it look sublime! But, with your permission," added the old gentleman courteously, "I will finish my story of the brig's escape.

"After we passed all the ice, the wind came round, as the captain said it would, right favourable for our course; and the *Cranky Jane* behaved like a good one. We made all our easting on one tack, and passed the Cape still a good distance to the south, but in as good a latitude as we could have passed it in for the weather we had, which was first-rate.

"And when we began to mount northwards again, towards the little island which we all prize so much, although it is but a little spot on the map of Europe, why, the wind changed too, still almost due aft as the dear old *Cranky Jane* liked, much to the delight and joy of everybody on board, especially the skipper, who exclaimed, as he rubbed his hands together in joy, and walked up and down the poop,—

"'Bless the darling, she's a walker! And I wouldn't swop her for the best clipper in the China trade!'

"We had a good land-fall all right, entering the Channel shortly after sighting the

Lizard, making the quickest passage ever known for a sailing brig from Fiji; and, in spite of all the dear old craft's shortcomings and temper and weather-helm, myself and the rest of the crew, including of course Pat O'Brien and his 'poor feet,' were willing, even after all the perils we had passed through, and the dangers we had escaped, every mother's son of us, with Captain Jiggins' permission, and the chief officer's favour, to sign articles, and ship for another voyage in the old *Cranky Jane*; and, what is more, we did too, sticking to the brig till she went to pieces off Cape Lewis to the south of New Zealand in her last voyage out. That's all!"

So saying, the old gentleman, bowing to me politely, took his departure from Sheerness dockyard, which I also left soon afterwards, pleased with all that I had seen and more than glad of having visited the place if only for the chance it afforded me of hearing this yarn.

THE GREEK BANDIT.

THE GREEK BANDIT.

A REMINISCENCE OF A YACHTING CRUISE IN THE ÆGEAN SEA.

SOME few years ago, when I was a youngster, I had what was then the great desire of my heart gratified by being allowed to accompany a party on a yachting cruise to the Mediterranean.

How I enjoyed myself, and how tragically our cruise nearly terminated, I will now proceed to tell.

There were six of us in all on board the yacht. There was dad, one; Captain Buncombe, two; Mr. Joe Moynham, three; Bob, four; myself, Charley, five; and dog Rollo, six—though I think, by rights, I ought to have counted Rollo first, as he was the best of us all, and certainly thought the least of himself—brave, fine, black, curly old fellow that he was!

Just as you fellows in England were having the nastiest part of the winter, when there is no skating or snowballing, and only drenching rain and easterly winds, that bring colds and coughs and mumps, we were enjoying the loveliest of blue skies and jolly warm weather, that made swimming in the sea a luxury, and ices after dinner seem like a taste of nectar. We did enjoy ourselves; and had a splendid cruise up the old Mediterranean, going everywhere and seeing everything that was to be seen. Oh, it was jolly! The yacht stopped at Gibraltar, where we climbed the rock and saw the monkeys that lived in the caverns on the top; at Malta, where we went up the "Nothing to Eat" stairs mentioned in *Midshipman Easy;* and then, sailing up the Levant, the *Moonshine* —she was eighty tons, and the crack of the R. Y. S.—was laid up at anchor for a long time at Alexandria, while we went ashore, going through the Suez Canal, across the desert to Cairo, and thence to the pyramids, after which we started for Greece.

You must know, before we get any further, that Bob and I didn't want to go anywhere near Greece at all! We had good reasons for this dislike. There were dad and Captain Buncombe—who was what people call an archæologist, fond of grubbing up old stones and skeletons, and digging like an old mole amongst ruins—continually talking all day long about Marathon and Hymettus, the Parthenon and Chersonese, the Acropolis, and Theseus and Odysseus and all the rest of them, bothering our lives out with questions about Homer and the *Iliad*, and all such stuff; so, I put it to you candidly, whether it wasn't almost as bad as being back again at school, making a fellow feel small who was shaky in his Greek and had a bad memory for history?

However, we had scarcely anchored in the Piræus when some events happened which drove the classics out of the heads of our elders; and I may say that thenceforth we heard no more about the ancients.

There had been a sharp squall shortly before, in which we had been amused by seeing the smart little xebeques, with their snowy white lateen sails, flying before the wind like a flock of small birds frightened by a hawk; and the *Moonshine* was just coming up to the wind in order to let go her anchor, when Bob and I, who were close together on the forecastle, watching the men preparing for running out and bitting the cable, saw, almost at the same moment, a man's head in the water right in front of the yacht's forefoot; then—it all happened as suddenly as a flash of lightning—his hands were thrown up as if in entreaty, although we heard no cry, and he disappeared.

"Man overboard!" sang out one of the crew, who was pulling away at the jib downhaul in order to stow the sail, the halliards having been cast loose. "Man overboard!" in a voice which rang through the vessel fore and aft, and attracted everybody's attention.

"Hi! Rollo, good dog!" cried out Bob, turning round sharp to where the brave old fellow had been lying on the deck not a moment before, flopping his tail lazily, and with his great red tongue lolling out, as though he laughed cheerily at everything going on around him.

"Hi! Rollo!" said I too, in almost the same breath with Bob. "Fetch him out, good dog!" and I turned round also.

But the dog was gone.

Bob and I were "nonplussed." We had both seen Rollo there not—why, not a second before. And now he was gone.

However, we soon discovered the noble fellow and the cause of his absence.

The cry of "Man overboard!" had startled everybody, so that the anchor had not been let go; and the steersman's attention, naturally, having been taken up, the yacht had paid off again instead of bringing up, and her head had swung; consequently, what had been ahead of us just before was now astern, and we were quite confused as to our bearings.

While we were looking in perplexity in every direction but the right one, Captain Buncombe, who was at the wheel, and perhaps anxious to atone for his carelessness in letting the *Moonshine* swing round, shouted out "Bravo!" waving his hat like a madman. Of course all our several pairs of eyes were turned on him at once.

"There he is—there he is—the brave old fellow!" cried the captain, letting go the helm in his eagerness, and pointing with his hat-waving hand to the water under the stern. "Look aft, you duffers! Where are your eyes? Bravo, Rollo! good dog! Hold up, old fellow! I'm coming to help you!" and with these words, before you could say "Jack Robinson," Captain Buncombe had thrown off his coat, pitched away the hat he had been waving, jumped over the taffrail of the yacht into the bosom of the blue Ægean Sea, and was rapidly swimming to where we could see dear old Rollo's black head and splashing paws as he supported a man in the yacht's wake, and tried to drag him towards us in the *Moonshine.*

We gave a "Hooray!" which you might have heard at Charing Cross if you had been listening!

Captain Buncombe and Rollo, with their burden, were so near the yacht that there was no necessity for lowering the gig as we had hastened to do; and in a very little time we hauled them on board—Rollo jumping about in the highest spirits, as if he had been just having a quiet lark on his own account; but the rescued person was limp and insensible, though he presently came to by the aid of hot-water bottles and blankets. The *Moonshine* then made another start, and succeeded better in anchoring in a respectable fashion, as she had always been accustomed to do.

The man was a handsome young fellow, with black hair and piercing eyes—a Greek, he told us in French which he spoke fluently —although he had not that treacherous cast of countenance which most of his countrymen possess. He was profuse in the thanks which he bestowed broadcast for our saving him from drowning, although Rollo had really all the credit of it. His name was Stephanos Pericles, he said, and he was crossing to Salamis, when the squall came on, and his boat was upset. He had been dragged under water by the boat and almost suffocated before he could get to the surface, being quite exhausted when the dog gripped him. For Rollo had seen him before any of us, and had not waited for our directions as to what to do.

"I'm a soldier," he said, proudly tapping his chest, and looking round at dad and the captain, and Mr. Moynham. "I've eaten your bread,"—he had dinner with us after he had got all right again, and we had settled down into that general routine in which our meals were attended to with the strictest punctuality—"and I shall never forget you have saved my life. By that bread I have eaten, I will repay you, I swear!"

Then turning to Bob and I, who were sitting on each side of him, and Rollo, who stuck close to him, as if under the idea that having saved him he was now his property—

"And much thanks to you, little Englishmen, and your dogs I vill nevare forget, no nevare!"

He couldn't speak English as well as French.

The evening had closed now, so Captain Buncombe told the crew to get the boat ready, and the Greek with many more fervent expressions of gratitude, was rowed ashore.

The next morning we had landed and after pottering about the port proceeded up to Athens, which much disappointed all of us, especially dad and the captain. It had a garish and stucco-like appearance; while the people looked as if they were costumed for a fancy ball, being not apparently at home in their national dress, picturesque though it was. It was quite nightmarish for Bob and me to read the names on the shop fronts in the streets, and see the newspapers printed in the old Greek characters. Fancy "Modiste," and "Perruquier," as they will have the French terms spelt, in the letters sacred to Euripides and Xenophon. It seemed like walking in a dream!

We had inspected Athens, as I've said, and visited the plain of Marathon, which was offered by the Greeks to Lord Byron for sixteen thousand piastres, or about eight hundred pounds—alas for glory!—and returned on board the yacht for dinner again, when we were told that a messenger had been off in our absence and left a parcel for us. What do you think it contained? Guess.

Well, there was a splendid shawl, worth more than a hundred guineas, for Captain Buncombe, and a handsome jewelled pipe for dad; while Mr. Joe Moynham had a case of Greek wines for his special self!

Bob and I were not forgotten either. He had a fine gun, with the stock inlaid with ivory, and carved beautifully; and I, a yataghan, decorated with a jewelled hilt, that was even more valuable than dad's pipe. Rollo was presented with a grand gold collar, which Mr. Joe Moynham said was like the one that Malachi, one of the Irish kings, wore in the days of Brian Boru; and, if you please, a lot of little purses, each containing a handsome present, were sent also in the parcel—a good big one, you may be sure—for distribution amongst the crew. It was princely gratitude, wasn't it, in spite of the slighting way in which Mr. Moynham had spoken of the modern Greeks and their ways? However, he had to "take it all back," as he said, when he drank the health of Monsieur Pericles—who seemed, by the way, to be much better off than his illustrious ancestor, and whom we put down as the Sultan Haroun el Raschid in disguise—in a glass of the very wine that he had sent on board the yacht.

But, that wasn't the end of it all, by any means:—why, I am only just coming to my real story now.

Time rolled on—when I say "time," of course, I only mean hours and days as we mean, not years and centuries as the ancients calculated the lapse of time—and we managed to see everything that sight-seers see in the city of Minerva.

Having nothing else to look at close at hand, therefore, we determined to go on our travels, like Ulysses; not amongst the islands, which we had already visited, but towards the mountains, Captain Buncombe having made a vow ere he left England to see the ruins of Thebes, after which, he said, he would have no further object in life, and would perform the Japanese feat of the "happy despatch!"

We had horses, and mules, and donkeys for the journey; that is, dad and the captain rode horses, there were mules for our traps and food, which we had to take along with us, thanks to the hospitality of the regions we were going to, while the donkeys were for Bob and me and Mr. Moynham. That gentleman, who would be very positive when he liked, declared that no earthly consideration should compel him to mount the Bucephalus that was provided for him. He said that a horse was expressly stated by King David to be "a vain thing to save a man," and so why should he go against that ruling?

The first part of our journey went off as jolly as possible: the way was good; the scenery—although I confess I didn't trouble my head very much about it, though dad and the captain were in raptures with it—magnificent; the halts, just at the right time, although all in classic places, whose names Bob and I hated the sound of; the food was first-rate, and Mr. Moynham so funny, that he nearly made me roll off my donkey every now and then with laughter. But towards evening, when we were all ascending a steep hill, with rocks and thick shrubbery on each side of it, through a narrow defile, a harsh voice suddenly exclaimed through the gloom, something that sounded like the Greek imperative Σταθητε, *Stop!* and then again another monosyllable, which we certainly understood better, "Halt!" A gun was also fired off at the same time; and, by the flash of the discharge we could see several long gleaming rifle barrels peering out from the bushes on either side of the way

"Brigands!" ejaculated the guides together, tumbling prostrate on the ground pell-mell, as if they had been swept down.

"Fascia a terra! Ventre à terre!" shouted out the same hoarse voice again, and a volley was fired over our heads.

"Pleasant!" said Mr. Moynham, throwing himself down with his face to the ground like the cowardly guides. "But I suppose we'd better do as these gentry require, or else they'll be hitting us under the fifth button-hole; and, what would become of us then?"

"Fascia a terra!" repeated the leader of the brigands, emerging from a clump of shrubbery at the head of the pass, motioning his arms violently at dad and the captain, who were inclined to show fight at first; but discretion proved the better part of valour, and they both dropped the pistols they had hurriedly drawn from their pockets, seeing that the rifle barrels covered them, sinking down prone on the earth like the rest of us.

Rollo, however, poor brave old fellow, made one dash at the ruffian as he threatened dad; and, seizing him by the throat, dashed him to the ground.

Poor fellow, the next moment he had a stiletto jammed into him, which made him sink down bleeding, with a faint howl, to which Bob and I responded with a cry, as if we felt the blow ourselves!

The moment dad and Captain Buncombe heard Rollo's howl and our cry, they jumped up again like lightning, and began hitting out right and left at the brigands who now surrounded us; and Mr. Moynham was not behind, I can tell you! He butted one big chap right in the pit of the stomach, and sent him tumbling down the defile, his body rattling against the stones, and he swearing like mad all the time. Bob and I scrambled at them as best we could, catching hold of their legs and tripping them up; but they were too many for us, for the cowardly guides did not stir hand or foot to help us, but lay stretched like logs along the ground, although they were unbound. We were certain that they were in league with the robbers; and so, without doubt, they were, for, if they had only assisted us, now that their assailants had dropped their firearms, and were engaged in a regular rough-and-tumble fight, we could have mastered them, I'm sure, as, counting Bob and myself in, we were nearly man for man as many as they were.

The struggle did not last long, although dad and the captain held out bravely to the last, flooring the brigands one after another, and knocking them down as if they had been nine-pins. They were presently tied securely, with their arms behind them, and menaced with death if they stirred, by a brawny ruffian touching each of their heads with a pistol barrel. As for Bob and me, they did not think it necessary to tie us.

"Well, this is a delightful ending to our picnic," said Mr. Moynham in lugubrious tones, as we all lay on the ground, with the exception of the guides, who appeared to mingle freely with the robbers, who were grouped in picturesque attitudes around us, leaning on their carbines. "I wonder what's their little game?"

The leader presently gave an order, and our seniors were then each lifted on to a horse or mule, and tied securely there.

"At all events," said Mr. Moynham, who kept up his spirits still wonderfully, "we sha'n't fall off, that's one comfort, and so we'll have the less bruises after the scrimmage!"

Although the chief brigand scowled at me, he allowed me to lift poor Rollo, who was not dead as I had feared, and I bandaged his neck where the wound was with my handkerchief, and took him up in front of me.

The leader then spoke vehemently in his own language to one of the treacherous guides, who approached dad as if to speak.

"Away, scoundrel!" said dad, wrathfully. "Don't speak to me; I would kill you if I were free, for leading us into this ambush!"

The man, however, urged again by the chief, who raised his pistol ominously at dad, approached him once more.

"The Albanian chief says that if twenty thousand piastres apiece, or one hundred thousand piastres in all, are not paid for you by sunset here to-morrow evening, you shall all be shot in cold blood, and your doom be on your own heads."

"Tell your chief, or thief, or whatever ruffian he is, that none of us will pay a penny. Our friends at Athens will miss us, and you'll have the palikari after you all in hot haste if I'm not back to-night safe."

"The English lord forgets that he left word that he might remain for two days on the mountains, and his friends will not think him missing before to-morrow night: at that time, the English lord and his friends, and the little lords, will be all dead men if the ransom be not paid."

"What on earth shall I do, Buncombe?" asked dad of the captain. "Shall I write an order on my bankers for the money to be sent? One hundred thousand piastres will be about five thousand pounds—I don't know whether my credit will be good for that amount?"

"Your credit and mine will be sufficient," Captain Buncombe said; "one can't trifle with these fellows, for the villains keep their word, I'm told."

The guide again spoke by the chief's order to dad, as if the tenor of the captain's words were understood.

"The Albanian chief declares that if the ransom be not paid by sunset to-morrow at latest, every one of you shall be shot, and your heads cut off and sent back to Athens in token of your fate."

"Ugh!" said Mr. Moynham, shuddering; "I certainly have been a Tory throughout all my life, but I should not like to follow Charles the First's example."

"I declare it's disgraceful," said Captain Buncombe; "I'll apply to the ambassador. This brigandage is the curse of Greece. I'll—"

"That won't help us now," said dad. "I suppose we must write for the ransom, although under protests; for, however much we have to pay, we must remember that our lives are in jeopardy; and that's the main consideration."

The advice was good; so, a joint letter was despatched to certain influential friends, as well as dad's banker at Athens, urging that the ransom should be sent in a certain way, to be handed over, as the brigand chief arranged, as we were given up, so that there should be no treachery on either side. The false guides then went off cheerfully down hill towards the plains, whilst our cavalcade, encompassed by the brigands, moved towards those mountain fastnesses, "where they resided when they were at home," as Mr. Moynham said.

THE NATIVE COSTUME.

Up and down hill and dale, we seemed in the darkness to be penetrating miles into the country; until, at last, passing, as well as we could see from the gloom, which was almost impenetrable, through a narrow glen between steep peaks, we suddenly turned a corner of a projecting rock, and found ourselves on an elevated plateau on the top of the mountains, where a strange scene awaited us. A number of ruddy watch-fires were burning with red and smoky light, and around these sat, reclined, or moved about, in a variety of active employments, a number of dark forms, most of which were robust Arnauts, clad in their national dress, which in the distance is not unlike that seen among Highlandmen, consisting as it does of a snowy white kilt, green velvet jacket, and bright-coloured scarf wound round the waist. Here and there, the glare from the firelight was reflected from the barrels of guns, rifles, and matchlocks, which the owners were cleaning or examining; while, before several of the fires cooking operations were going on. Kids, whole sheep, and pieces of raw flesh, were being slowly broiled, hanging from bits of stick stuck in the ground, or suspended by pieces of string attached to the branches of the overhanging trees that encircled the plateau. This added to the "effect" of the scene.

"Quite operatic, and better than old Drury," I heard Mr. Moynham say; but we were all too depressed and uncomfortable from our constrained attitudes to feel inclined to appreciate the picturesque, the brigands having taken us off the horses, and flung us down on the ground, having this time bound even Bob and myself; indeed, they treated us with even less attention than they would have bestowed on anything eatable, judging by the care they evinced in their cuisine, although they did not offer us anything either to eat or drink, much to Mr. Moynham's great chagrin especially, nor did they give us the slightest covering to protect us from the night air when the waning watch-fires told us that bedtime—save the mark—had arrived. I suppose they thought that it did not much matter if we did catch cold, considering that we were going to be shot within twenty-four hours!

Tired out with fatigue, we finally sank to

rest in the same place where we were first pitched down, not awaking till late the next morning, when we found most of the brigands had departed—to look out for other "welcome guests" like ourselves, I suppose! Only three were left to guard us, but they were quite enough, considering that we were tied up fast, and couldn't move if we wished.

How slowly that day dragged out! We thought it would never end. They gave us some hard coarse dry bread to eat and water to drink, nothing else; and the hours dragged themselves slowly along, as if they would never end.

Our hopes gradually sank, as the sun declined in the heavens, for we watched the progress of the glowing orb with almost the devoted zeal of the followers of Zoroaster.

At last, just as it was within half an hour of sunset as nearly as we could calculate, we heard a tumult as of many voices in the ravine leading to the plateau; and, presently, the man whom we had conceived to be the leader of the brigands advanced towards us, in company with his band, now largely reinforced by others. At a word from him our bonds were untied, and we were assisted to our feet, on which we could not stand firmly for some little time, on account of the want of circulation of our blood during the long time we had been in such constrained attitudes.

The guide who had previously acted the part of interpreter after betraying us— although, by the way, he told us before he left us that he belonged to the band, and thus, perhaps, had only acted honourably according to his creed—then translated what the leader had to say.

Our ransom had been paid, and we were free to go down the mountains. The horses, mules, and everything belonging to us would be restored, and a trusty guide—the speaker, of course—would put us in the direct route to Athens, but as near the city as possible; and, finally, the chief begged that we would excuse the rough treatment to which we had been subjected, as he had a great regard for us!

"It was all very well to dissemble his love," quoted Mr. Moynham; "but,—why did he kick us down-stairs?"

"The chief!—which chief, or thief?" said dad sternly. He did not feel particularly pleased with the Arnauts or their leader. "I've had enough of the scoundrels already, and the sooner I lose sight of them the better! What do you mean by the chief?"

"He means me!" said a gorgeous individual, all green velvet jacket, and gold braid, and red sash, with a cap set rakishly on the side of his head in the front of which glittered a diamond of surpassing brilliancy.

We had noticed this individual before, but not especially, and he had been rather hidden by the figure of the man we looked upon as the leader: now he stepped forward, and we could see his face plainly, as we recognized the voice.

Who do you think it was?

Why, Stephanos Pericles, the man whom we had saved from drowning, and who had sent us those handsome presents!

"Why have we met with this treatment at your hands?" said papa, puzzled at the Greek's behaviour.

"You have nothing to complain of," said Stephanos, with an air of courteous nobility which exasperated the captain to that degree that I saw him clenching and unclenching his fists, and dancing about, as Mr. Moynham said afterwards, "like a hen on a hot griddle."

"My dear sir, you have nothing really to complain of," said the Greek. "You saved my life, I admit, and I think I politely expressed my obligations at the time. In return I now present you with five lives, independently of that of the dog, which, I am sorry to see, has been hurt."

"But the ransom?" said dad.

"Oh, I'm sorry I had to insist on that," said Stephanos, placidly; "but it is one of our rules to enforce such in all cases, and I'm sorry that I could not let you off, although my friendship yearned to set you free without it. You must really please excuse the treatment you have met with. If I had known who honoured me with their company, I'm sure you would have had no reason to be dissatisfied with my hospitality. The *next* time you favour me with your presence, my lord—"

"The next time you catch me here, or anywhere else on Greek ground," laughed my father in a hearty "Ho! ho!" in which all of us joined, "you may cut me up into kabobs and cook and eat me, and welcome; for I know I'll then deserve it!"

We got back safe aboard the *Moonshine* all right, setting sail from the Piræus next day; but it was a good trick of the brigand chief, wasn't it—though I can't say much for his gratitude after all, spite of those magnificent presents, which there was little reason to wonder at his offering us, considering the easy manner in which he got his money?

The cut in Rollo's neck healed soon, and he is now as right as ever he was, excepting a slight scar which tells where the stiletto or dagger went, and he wears still the collar of gold that Stephanos Pericles presented him with. As for the rest of our party, all of us got home safe with the *Moonshine*, which is now fitting out at Ryde for the coming regatta, where I hope she'll come off as successfully in carrying off prizes as "THE GREEK BANDIT."

JIM NEWMAN'S YARN.

JIM NEWMAN'S YARN:

OR,

A SIGHT OF THE SEA SERPENT.

"WAS you ever up the Niger, sir?"

"Why, of course not, Jim! you know that I've never been on the African station, or any other for that matter. But, why do you ask the question?"

"Don't know 'xactly, sir. P'raps that blessed sea-fog reminds me of it, somehow or other—though there's little likeness, as far as that goes, between the west coast and Portsmouth, is there, sir?"

"I don't suppose there is," I said; "but what puts the Niger, of all places in the world, in your head at the present moment?"

"Ah, that'd tell a tale, sir," he answered, cocking his left eye in a knowing manner, and giving the quid in his mouth a turn. "Ah, that'd tell a tale, sir!"

Jim Newman, an old man-of-war's man—now retired from the navy, and who eked out his pension by letting boats for hire to summer visitors—was leaning against an old coal barge that formed his "office," drawn up high and dry on the beach, midway between Southsea Castle and Portsmouth Harbour, and gazing out steadily across the channel of the Solent, to the Isle of Wight beyond. He and I were old friends of long standing, and I was never so happy as when I could persuade him—albeit it did not need much persuasion—to open the storehouse of his memory, and spin a yarn about his old experiences afloat in the whilom wooden walls of England, when crack frigates were the rage instead of screw steamers with armour-plates. We had been talking of all sorts of service gossip—the war, the weather, what not—when he suddenly asked me the question about the great African river that has given poor Sambo "a local habitation and a name."

Although the gushing tears of April had hardly washed away the traces of the wild March winds, the weather had suddenly become almost tropical in its heat. There was not the slightest breath of air stirring, and the sea lay lazily asleep, only throbbing now and then with a faint spasmodic motion, which barely stirred the shingle on the shore, much less plashed on the beach; while a thick, heavy white mist was steadily creeping up from the sea, shutting out, first the island, and then the roadstead at Spithead from view, and overlapping the whole landscape in thick woolly folds, moist yet warm. Jim had said that the sea-fog, coming as it did, was a sign of heat, and that we should have a regular old-fashioned hot summer, unlike those of recent years.

"Ah, sir," he repeated, "I could tell a tale about that deadly Niger river, and the Gaboon, and the whole treacherous coast, if I liked, from Lagos down to the Congo— ay, I could! It was that 'ere sea-fog that put Afriker into my head, Master Charles; I know that blessed white mist, a-rising up like a curtain, well, I do! The ' white man's shroud,' the niggers used to call it—and many a poor beggar it has sarved to shroud too, in that killing climate, confound it!"

"Well, Jim, tell us about the Niger to begin with," said I, so as to bring him up to the scratch without delay; for, when Jim once got on the moralizing or sentimental tack, he generally ended by getting angry with everybody and everything around him; and when he got angry, there was an end to his stories for that day at least.

"All right, your honour," said the old fellow, calming down at once into his usual serenity again, and giving his quid another shift as he braced himself well up against the old barge, on the half-deck of which I was seated with my legs dangling down—"All right, your honour! If it's a yarn you're after, why I had best weigh anchor at once and make an offing, or else we shan't be able to see a handspike afore us!"

"Heave ahead, Jim!" said I impatiently; "you are as long as a three-decker in getting under way!"

With this encouragement, he cleared his throat with his customary hoarse, choking sort of cough, like an old raven, and commenced his narrative without any further demur.

"It's more'n twenty years now since I left the service—ay, thirty years would be more like it; and almost my very last cruise was on the West African station. I had four years of it, and I recollect it well; for, before I left the blessed, murdering coast, with its poisonous lagoons covered with thick green slime, and sickly smells, and burning sands, I seed a sight there that I shall never forget as long as I live, and which would make me recklect Afrikey well enough if nothing else would!"

"That's right, Jim, fire away!" said I, settling myself comfortably on my seat to enjoy the yarn. "What was it that you saw?"

"Steady! Let her go easy, your honour; I'm a-coming to that soon enough. It was in the old *Amphitrite* I was at the time—she's broken up and burnt for firewood long ago, poor old thing!—and we was a-lying in the Bight of Benin, alongside of a slaver which we had captured the day before off

Whydah. She was a Brazilian schooner with nearly five hundred wretched creatures on board, so closely packed that you could not find space enough to put your foot fairly on her deck in any place. The slaves had only been a night on board her; but the stench was so awful, from so many unfortunate niggers being squeezed so tightly together like herrings in a barrel, and under a hot sun too, that we were longing to send the schooner away to Sierra Leone, and get rid of the horrid smell, which was worse than the swamps ashore! Well, I was in the morning watch after we had towed in the slaver to the Bights, having carried away her foremast with a round shot in making her bring to, and was just going forward to turn in as the next watch came on deck, when who should hail me but my mate, Gil Saul, coming in from the bowsprit, where he had been on the look-out —it was him as was my pardner here when I first started as a shore hand in letting out boats, but he lost the number of his mess long ago like our old ship the *Amphitrite*.

"As he came up to me his face was as

white as your shirt, and he was trembling all over as if he was going to have a fit of the fever and ague.

"'Lor', Gil Saul,' sez I, 'what's come over you, mate? are you going on the sick list, or what?'

"'Hush, Jim,' sez he, quite terror-stricken. 'Don't speak like that; I've seen a ghost, and I knows I shall be a dead man afore the day's out!'

"With that I burst into a larf.

"'Bless your eyes, Gil,' sez I, 'tell that to the marines, my bo'! you can't get over me on that tack. You won't find any respectable ghosts leaving dear old England for the sake of this dirty, sweltering west coast, which no Christian would come to from choice, let alone a ghost!'

"'But, Jim,' he sez, leaning his hand on my arm to detain me as I was going down below, 'this wasn't a h'English ghost as I sees just now. It was the most outlandish foreign reptile you ever see. A long, big, black snake like a crocodile, only twice the length of the old corvette; with a head like a bird, and eyes as big and fiery as our sidelights. It was a terrible creature, Jim, and its eyes flamed out like lightning, and it snorted like a horse as it swam by the ship. I've had a warning, old shipmate, and I'll be a dead man before to-morrow morning, I know!'

"The poor chap shook with fright as he spoke, though he was as brave a man as we had aboard; so I knew that he had been drinking and was in a state of delirium tremendibus, or else he was sickening for the African fever, which those who once have never forget. I therefore tried to pacify him and explain away his fancy.

"'That's a good un, Gil Saul,' I sez. 'Don't you let none of the other hands hear what you've told me, that you've seen the great sea sarpint, or you'll never get the end of it.'

"Gil got angry at this, forgetting his fright in his passion at my doubting his word like.

"'But it was the sea sarpint, I tells you, or its own brother if it wasn't. Didn't I see it with my own eyes, and I was as wide awake as you are, and not caulking?'

"'The sea sarpint!' I repeated scornfully, laughing again in a way that made Gil wild. 'Who ever heard tell of such a thing, except in a Yankee yarn?'

"'And why shouldn't there be a big snake in the sea the same as there are big snakes on land like the Bow constreetar, as is read of in books of history, Jim Newman? Some folks are so cocksure, that they won't believe nothing but what they sees for themselves. I wonder who at home, now, would credit that there are some monkeys here in Afrikey that are bigger than a man and walk upright; and you yourself, Jim, have told me that when you were in Australy you seed rabbits that were more than ten foot high when they stood on their hind-legs, and that could jump a hundred yards at one leap.'

"'So I have, Gil Saul,' sez I, a bit nettled at what he said, and the way he said it, 'and what I says I stick to. I have seen at Port Philip kangaroos, which are just like big rabbits with upright ears, as big as I've said; and I've seen 'em, too, jump more than twice the distance any horse could.'

"'And why then,' sez he, argumentifying

on to me like a shot, 'and why then shouldn't there be such a thing as the sea sarpint?'

"This flummuxed me a bit, for I couldn't find an answer handy, so I axed him another question to get out of my quandary.

"'But why, Gil, did you say you had seed a ghost, when it was a sarpint?'

"This time *he* was bothered for a moment.

"'Because, Jim,' sez he, after a while, 'it appeared so awful to me when I saw it coming out of the white mist with its glaring red eyes and terrible beak. It was a ghost I feels, if it wasn't the sea sarpint; and whether or no it bodes no good to the man wot sees it, I know. I'm a doomed man.'

"I couldn't shake him from that belief, though I thought the whole thing was fancy on his part, and I turned into my hammock soon after we got below, without a thought more about the matter—it didn't stop my caulk, I know. But, ah! that was only in the early morning. Before the day was done, as Gil had said, that conversation was recalled to me in a terrible way—ah, a terrible way!" the old sailor repeated impressively, taking off his tarpaulin hat, and wiping his forehead with his handkerchief, as if the recollection of the past awed him even now. He looked so serious that I could not laugh, inclined as I was to ridicule any such story as that of the fabled sea serpent, which one looks for periodically as a transatlantic myth to crop up in dull seasons in the columns of American newspapers.

"And did you see it too?" I asked; "and Gil Saul's prophecy turns out true?"

"You shall hear," he answered gravely; "I'm not spinning a yarn, as you call it, Master Charles; I'm telling you the truth."

"Go on, Jim," said I, to reassure him. "I'm listening, all attention."

"At eight bells that day, another man-of-war come in, bringing an empty slaver she had taken before she had shipped her cargo. In this vessel we were able to separate some of the poor wretches packed on board our Brazilian schooner, and so send them comfortably on to Sierra Leone, which was what we were waiting to do, as I've told you already; and now being free to go cruising again, we hove up anchor and made our way down the coast to watch for another slaver which we had heard news of by the man-o'-war that came in to relieve us.

"We had a spanking breeze all day, for a wonder, as it generally fails at noon; but towards the evening, when we had made some eighty miles or so from the Bights, it fell suddenly dead calm, as if the wind had been shut off slap without warning. It was bright before, but the moment the calm came a thick white mist rose around the vessel, just like that which came just now from seaward, and has hidden the island and Spithead from view; you see how it's reminded me now of the west coast and the Niger river, Master Charles, don't you?"

"Ay," said I, "Jim, I see what you were driving at."

"Those thick mists," he continued, "always rise on the shores of Afrikey in the early mornings—just as there was a thick one when Gil had seen his ghost, as he said—and they comes up again when the sun sets; but you never sees 'em when the sun's a-shining bright as it was that arternoon. It was the rummiest weather I ever see. By and by, the mist lifted a bit, and then there were clumps of fog dancing about on the surface of the sea, which was oily and calm, just like patches of trees on a lawn. Sometimes these fog curtains would come down and settle round the ship, so that you couldn't see to the t'other side of the deck for a minute, and they brought a fearful bad smell with them, the very smell of the lagoons ashore with a dash of the niggers aboard the slave schooner, only a thousand times worse, and we miles and miles away from the land. It was most unaccountable, and most uncomfortable. I couldn't make it out at all.

"Jest as I was a-puzzling my brains as to the reason of these fog banks and the stench they brought with them, Gil Saul came on deck too, and sheered up alongside of me as I was looking out over the side. His face was a worse sight than the morning; for, instead of his looking white, the colour of his skin was gray and ashy, like the face of a corpse. It alarmed me so that I cried out at once—

"'Go down below, Gil! Go down and report yourself to the doctor!'

"'No,' sez he, 'it ain't the doctor as will cure me, Jim; I feel it coming over me again as I felt this morning. I shall see that sarpint or ghost again, I feel sure.'

"What with his face and his words, and the bad smell from the fog, I confess I began to feel queer myself—not frightened exactly—but I'd have much rather have been on Southsea common in the broad daylight than where I was at that moment, I can tell you."

"Did you see anything, Jim?" I asked the old sailor at this juncture.

"I seed nothing, Master Charles, *as yet*; but I felt something, I can't tell what or how to explain; it was a sort of all-overish feeling, as if something was a-walking over my grave, as folks say, summat uncanny, I do assure you.

"The captain and the first lieutenant was on the quarter-deck, the latter with his telescope to his eye a-gazing at something forward apparently, that he was trying to discern amongst the clumps of fog. I was nigh them, and being to leeward could hear what they said.

"The first lieutenant, I hears him, turns to

the captain over his shoulder speaking like, and sez he—

"'Captain Manter, I can't make it out exactly, but it's most curious;' and then turning to me, he sez, 'Newman, go down to my steward and ax him to give you my night-glass.'

"I went down and fetched the glass and handed it to him, he giving me t'other one to hold; and he claps the night-glass to his eye.

"'By Jove, Captain Manter,' sez he presently, 'I was right, it is the greatest marine monster I ever saw!'

"'Pooh!' says the captain, taking the glass from him and looking himself. 'It's only a waterspout, they come sometimes along with this appearance of the sea!' But presently I heard him mutter something under his voice to the lieutenant, and then he said aloud, 'It is best to be prepared;' and a moment after that he gave an order, and the boatswain piped up and we beat to quarters. It was very strange that, wasn't it? And so every man on board thought.

"A very faint breeze was springing up

again, and I was on the weather side of the ship, which was towards the land from which the wind came, when suddenly Gil Saul, who was in the same battery and captain of my crew, grips my arm tight. 'It's coming! it's coming!' he said right in my ear, and then the same horrible foul smell wafted right over the ship again, and a noise was heard just as if a herd of wild horses were sucking up water together.

"At this moment the fog lifted for a bit, and we could see clear for about a couple of miles to windward, where the captain and first lieutenant and all the hands had their eyes fixed as if expecting something.

"By George! you could have knocked me down with a feather, I tell you! I never saw such a sight in my life, and may I never see such another again! There, with his head well out of the water, shaped like a big bird, and higher in the air than the main truck of the ship, was a gigantic reptile like a sarpint, only bigger than you ever dreamt of. He was wriggling through the water at a fearful rate, and going nearly the same course as ourselves, with a wake behind him bigger than a line-of-battle ship with paddle-wheels, and his length—judging by what I saw of him—was about half a mile at least, not mentioning what part of his body was below the water; while he must have been broader across than the largest sperm whale, for he showed good five feet of freeboard.

"The captain and first lieutenant were flabbergasted, I could see; but Captain Manter was as brave an officer as ever stepped, and he pulled himself together in a minute, as the fog, which had only lifted for a minute, came down again shutting out everything from view so that we could not see a yard from the side. 'Don't be alarmed, my men,' he sings out in his cheery voice, so that every hand could hear him, 'it's only a waterspout that is magnified by the fog; and as it gets nearer we'll give it the starboard broadside to clear it up and burst it.'

"'Ay! ay!' sez the men with a cheer, while the smell grew more awful and the snorting gushing sound we had heard before so loud that it was quite deafening, just immediately after the captain spoke, when it had stopped awhile.

"As for poor Gil, he had never lost the grip of my arm since we sighted the reptile, although he had the lanyard of his gun in his right hand all the same.

"'Fire!' sez the captain; and, in a moment, the whole starboard broadside was fired off, point blank across the water, in a line with the deck, as Captain Manter had ordered us to depress the guns, the old *Amphitrite* rocking to her keel with the explosion.

"Well, sir, as true as I'm standing here a-talking to you, at the very instant the guns belched out their fire and smoke, and the cannon-balls with which they were loaded, there was a most treemenjus roar and a dash of water alongside the ship, and the waves came over us as if we were on a lee shore; and then, as the men stood appalled at the things going on around them, which was what no mortal ever seed before, Gil clasped my arm more tightly, loosening his right hand from the lanyard of the gun which he had now fired, and shrieked out, 'There! there!'

"Master Charles, it were awful! A long heavy body seemed to be reared up high in the air right athwart the vessel, and plunged far away in the sea to leeward; and, as the body passed over our heads, I looked up with Gil, and saw the fearful fiery eyes of the biggest snake that ever crawled on the earth, though this was flying in the air, and round his hideous head, that had a long beak like a bird, was a curious fringe or frill all yellowish green, just like what a lizard puffs out under his throat when in a rage. I could see no more, for the thing was over us and gone a mile or more to leeward in a wink of the eye, the fog drifting after it and hiding it from sight. Besides which, I was occupied with Gil, who had sank down on the deck in a dead swoon.

"Whatever it was, the thing carried away our main topmast with the yards, and everything clean from the caps as if it had been shot away, and there wasn't a trace of them floating in the sea around, as we could see.

"'A close thing that!' said the captain, after the shock was over, speaking to the lieutenant, although all hands could hear him, for it was as still as possible now. 'A close thing, Mr. Freemantle. I've known a waterspout do even more damage than this; so let us be thankful!'

"And then all hands were piped to clear the wreck, and make the ship snug; for we had some bad weather afterwards, and had to put into Sierra Leone to refit.

"Gil was in a swoon for a long time after; and then he took the fever bad, and only recovered by the skin of his teeth; but he never forgot what he had seen, nor I either, nor any of the hands, though we never talked about it. We knew we had seen something unearthly; even the captain and Lieutenant Freemantle, though they put down the damage to a waterspout for fear of alarming the men, knew differently, as we did. We had seen the great sea sarpint, if anybody had, every man-jack of us aboard! It was a warning, too, as poor Gil Saul had declared; for, strange to say, except himself and me, not a soul as was on board the *Amphitrite* when the reptile overhauled us, lived to see Old England again. The bones of all the others were left to bleach on the burning sands of the east coast of Africa, which has killed ten thousand more of our own countrymen with its deadly climate than we have saved slaves from slavery!"

"But, Jim," said I, as the old sailor paused at the end of his yarn. "Do you think it was really the sea serpent? Might it not have been a waterspout, or a bit of floating wreck, which you saw in the fog?"

Jim Newman got grumpy at once, at the bare insinuation of such a thing.

"Waterspouts and bits of wreck," said he sarcastically, "generally travel at the rate of twenty miles an hour when there is no wind to move them along, and a dead calm, don't they? Waterspouts and bits of wreck smell like polecats when you're a hundred miles from land, don't they? Waterspouts and bits of wreck roar like a million wild bulls, and snort and swish as they go through the water like a thousand express trains going through a tunnel, don't they?"

I was silenced by Jim's sarcasm, and humbly begged his pardon for doubting the veracity of his eyesight.

"Besides, Master Charles," he urged, when he had once more been restored to his usual equanimity; "besides, you must remember that nearly in the same parts, and about the same time—in the beginning of the month of August, 1848—the sea sarpint, as people who have never seen it are so fond of joking of, was seen by the captain and crew of H.M.S. *Dædalus* and the event was put down in the ship's log, and reported officially to the Admiralty. I suppose you won't go for to doubt the statement which was made by a captain in the navy, a gentleman, and a man of honour, and supported by the evidence of the lieutenant of the watch, the master, a midshipman, the quartermaster, boatswain's mate, and the man at the wheel—the rest of the ship's company being below at the time?"

"No, Jim," said I, "that's straight enough."

"We was in latitude 5° 30′ N., and longitude about 3° E.," continued the old sailor, "when we saw it on the 1st of August, 1848, and they in latitude 24° 44′ S., and longitude 9° 22′ E., when they saw it on the 6th of the same month; so the curious reptile—for reptile he was—must have put the steam on when he left us!"

"Stirred up, probably, by your starboard broadside?" said I.

"Jest so," went on Jim. "But, he steered just in the direction to meet them when he went off from us, keeping a southward and eastward course; and I daresay, if he liked, he could have made a hundred knots an hour as easy as we could sail ten on a bowline with a stiff breeze."

"And so you really have seen the great sea serpent?" said I, when the old man-of-war's man had shifted his quid once more, thus implying that he had finished.

"Not a doubt of it, sir; and by the same token he was as long as from here to the Spit Buoy, and as broad as one of them circular forts out there."

"That's a very good yarn, Jim," said I; "but do you mean to say that you saw the monster with your own eyes, Jim, as well as all the rest of you?"

"I saw him, I tell you, Master Charles, as plain as I see you now; and as true as I am standing by your side the sarpint jumped right over the *Amphitrite* when Gil Saul and I was a-looking up, and carried away our maintopmast and everything belonging to it!"

"Well, it must have been wonderful, Jim," said I.

"Ay, ay, sir," said he, "but you'd ha' thought it a precious sight more wonderful if you had chanced to see it, like me!"

I may add, that, shortly afterwards, I really took the trouble to overhaul a pile of the local papers to see whether Jim's account of the report made by the captain of the *Dædalus* to the Lords of the Admiralty was substantially true; and, strange to say, I discovered amongst the numbers of the *Hampshire Telegraph* for the year 1848, the following copy of a letter forwarded by Captain M'Quhae to the admiral in command at Devonport dockyard at the date mentioned:—

"Her Majesty's Ship *Dædalus*,
"Hamoaze, Oct. 11th, 1848.

"Sir,—In reply to your letter of this day's date, requiring information as to the truth of a statement published in the *Globe* newspaper, of a sea serpent of extraordinary dimensions having been seen from her Majesty's ship *Dædalus*, under my command, on her passage from the East Indies, I have the honour to acquaint you, for the information of my Lords Commissioners of the Admiralty, that at five o'clock, p.m., on the 6th of August last, in latitude 24° 44' S., and longitude 9° 22′ E., the weather dark and cloudy, wind fresh from the N.W., with a long ocean swell from the S.W., the ship on the port tack heading N.E. by N., something very unusual was seen by Mr. Sartoris, midshipman, rapidly approaching the ship from before the beam. The circumstance was immediately reported by him to the officer of the watch, Lieut. Edgar Drummond, with whom and Mr. Wm. Barrett, the master, I was at the time walking the quarter-deck. The ship's company were at supper.

"On our attention being called to the object it was discovered to be an enormous serpent, with head and shoulders kept about four feet constantly above the surface of the sea, and as nearly as we could approximate by comparing it with the length of what our maintopsail-yard would show in the water, there was at the very least sixty feet of the animal *à fleur d'eau*, no portion of which was, to our perception, used in propelling it through the water, either by vertical or horizontal undulation. It passed rapidly, but so close under our lee quarter that had it been a man of my acquaintance I should have easily recognized his features with the naked eye; and it did not, either in approaching the ship or after it had passed our wake, deviate in the slightest degree from its course to the S.W., which it held on at the pace of from twelve to fifteen miles per hour, apparently on some determined purpose.

"The diameter of the serpent was about fifteen or sixteen inches behind the head, which was, without any doubt, that of a snake, and never, during the twenty minutes that it continued in sight of our glasses once below the surface of the water; its colour a dark brown, with yellowish white about the throat. It had no fins, but something like the mane of a horse, or rather a bunch of sea-weed, washed about its back. It was seen by the quartermaster, the boatswain's mate, and the man at the wheel, in addition to myself and officers above-mentioned.

"I am having a drawing of the serpent made from a sketch taken immediately after it was seen, which I hope to have ready for transmission to my Lords Commissioners of the Admiralty by to-morrow's posts.

"I have, &c.,

"PETER M'QUHAE, Captain.

"To Admiral Sir W. H. Gage, G.C.H., Devonport."

Consequently, having this testimony, which was amply verified by the other witnesses at the time, I see no reason to doubt the truth of Jim Newman's yarn about THE GREAT SEA SERPENT!

"OUR SCRATCH ELEVEN."

"OUR SCRATCH ELEVEN."

THIS all happened a year or two before I went to sea, and so doesn't come under the ordinary designation of a "yarn," which, I take it, should only be about the doings of seafaring men and those who have to toil over the ocean for a living; still, as it concerns myself, I give it in pretty nearly the exact words I told it the other day to a party of youngsters who had just come in from cricketing and asked me for a story.

I never played in such a match in my life before or since, I began; but, there, I had better commence at the right end, and then you'll be able to judge for yourselves.

Charley Bates, of course, was dead against it from the first.

"I tell you it's all nonsense," he said, when we mooted the subject to him. "How on earth can we get up a decent eleven to play chaps like those, who have been touring it all over the country, and licking professionals even on their own ground? It's impossible, and a downright absurdity. We can't do it."

"But, Charley," suggested Sidney Grant, a tall, fair-haired fellow, and our best bat— he could swipe away at leg balls; and as for straight drives, well, he'd send 'em over a bowler's head, just out of his reach, and right to the boundary wall, at such a rate, like an express train going through the air, that they defied stopping. "But, Charley," he suggested, "we've got some good ones left of our team, and I daresay we can pick up some fresh hands from amongst the visitors to make up a fair scratch lot."

"It would be a scratch lot," sneered Charley—"a lot that would be scratched out with duck's eggs, and make us the laughing-stock of the place."

"Oh, that's all nonsense!" Sidney said, decisively.

Besides being our best bat, he was the captain of the Little Peddlington Cricket Club, which, as it was far into the month of August, had got somewhat dispersed through some of the team having gone off on those cheap excursions to London, to the Continent, and elsewhere, that are rife at most of the seaside places on the south coast during the season. But now that the great travelling team of the "Piccadilly Inimitables" purposed paying a passing visit to our rural shades, it of course behoved the Little Peddlington Cricket Club to challenge the celebrated amateurs to a match, albeit we were so woefully weak from the absence of many of our best members, or else be for ever disgraced amongst the patrons of the noble game.

It was this very point we were debating now, our captain having collected the remnants of the club together in solemn caucus, to deliberate on the situation and see what was to be done.

"I don't see why we shouldn't challenge the Inimitables," he went on. "The worst that can happen to us is to get licked; but we might make a good fight for it, and if vanquished we should not be covered with dishonour. There are five of us here of the first eleven to form a nucleus with: Charley Bates—whom I mention first, not by reason of his superior skill with the willow," the captain slily put in, "as that is known to all of us, but on account of his being the oldest member of the Little Peddlington Cricket Club present, with the exception of myself— Jack Limpet, who is a very good all-round player if he didn't brag quite so much,"— this was one at me—" Tom Atkins, John Hardy, and last, though by no means least, my worthy self. Thus we've five good men and true, whom we have tried already in many a fray, to rely on; and I daresay we can pick out two or three likely youngsters from the juniors, while some of those new fellows amongst the visitors that came down last week would lend us a hand. There were three of them especially that I noticed yesterday practising, whom I should certainly like to have in the eleven if I could get them to join us."

"They'd be glad enough if you'd ask

them," grumbled Charley Bates, who always seemed to prefer looking at the disagreeable side of things; "but I don't think much of their play. And as for the juveniles, there isn't one worth his salt."

"Yes, there is," said John Hardy, who seldom spoke; but when he did open his mouth, generally did so to the purpose. "That young fellow James Black is first class both at batting and bowling. I've watched him many a time. He ought to have been in the eleven long ago."

"Do you think so?" said Sidney inquiringly. "I'm afraid I've overlooked him. I'll make a note of his name, even if we don't have him with us to play against the Inimitables."

Without much further demur, Sidney Grant proceeded to settle that he and John Hardy should form themselves into a deputation and wait upon the committee of the visitors' cricket club, requesting them to furnish the assistance of the three members whom our captain had specified, to the Little Peddlington Eleven, which would be also duly recruited from the ranks of its junior team, not forgetting young James Black, in order to enable them to challenge the Piccadilly Inimitables, and try to stop their triumphal progress round the south coast.

Charley Bates objected, naturally, as might have been imagined from the position he took at first. He objected not only to the visitors being asked to join our scratch team and represent the Little Peddlingtonians, but also specially—just because John Hardy mentioned his name, and for no other earthly reason—to the fact of young Black's being selected from the junior eleven. He was overruled, however, on both points, much to his chagrin, as he was in the habit generally of getting his own way by bullying the rest, and he left the meeting in the greatest disgust, saying that he wouldn't play, and thus "make himself a party to the disgrace that was looming over the club," in their defeat by the Inimitables, which he confidently expected.

"He's too fond of figuring in public to care to take a back seat when we are all in it, and bite off his nose to spite his face!" said Tom Atkins when he went away from us in his dudgeon, shaking off the dust from his cricketing shoes, so to speak, in testimony against us. "Master Charley will come round and join us when he sees we are in for the match, you bet!"

And so he did, at the last moment.

The other members having cordially supported the captain's several propositions, they were carried unanimously by our quorum of four, and immediately acted upon. Young Black, with two other juniors, and three of the best men we could pick out from the visitors that were at Little Peddlington for the season that year—and there were some first-rate cricketers, too, amongst them—made up our scratch eleven, Charley Bates relenting when he found that we would have played without him. And a challenge having been sent to the Piccadilly Inimitables without delay, which they as promptly accepted, the match was fixed to come off, on our ground, of course, on the opening days of the ensuing week—provided, as the secretary of our opponents' club, very offensively as we thought, added in a postscript to his communication, the contest was not settled on the first day's play. But they reckoned without their host when they tackled the Little Peddlingtonians, as you will see.

We fellows who formed the Little Peddlington Cricket Club were for the most part studying there under a noted tutor, who prepared us for the army, Woolwich, or India; but we admitted a few of the townspeople.

A cricket match at such a retired spot opened a field of excitement to both residents and summer tourists alike. Even an ordinary contest, such as we sometimes indulged in with the Hammerton or Smithwick clubs, or the Bognor garrison, would have aroused considerable interest in the vicinity of Little Peddlington; but when it became known that we were going to play the celebrated Piccadilly Inimitables, who had licked Lancashire and Yorkshire, and almost every county eleven they had met in their cricketing tour from the north to the south of England, there was nothing else talked about from one end of our seaside town to the other, the news spreading to the adjacent hamlets, and villages beyond, until it reached the cathedral city twenty miles away.

THE BATTLE BEGINS.

Under these circumstances it cannot be wondered at that when Monday, the opening day of the match—which turned out beautifully fine for a wonder, as it always rained on the very slightest provocation at Little Peddlington—arrived, there was such a crowd of carriages and drags, filled to their utmost capacity, as to astonish even the memory of that far-famed individual " the oldest inhabitant." These were drawn up in a sort of semicircle around our cricket ground—a charmingly situated spot with a very wide area, and nicely sheltered by rows of waving elms from the hot August sun—and besides the " carriage folk," as the rustics termed them, came on foot everybody in the neighbourhood, besides all Little Peddlington itself.

The Piccadilly Inimitables arrived early in the morning, having stopped overnight at Brighton, where they had scored their last victory over the Sussex eleven, and which place was not so remote from Little Peddlington as you might suppose, consequently we were able to commence the match in good time, and as our club won the toss for first innings we buckled to at once for the fray, sending in John Hardy, who had the reputation with us of being a "sticker," and the grumbling Charley Bates, to the wickets punctually at eleven o'clock.

The bowling at the beginning was rather shady, the Inimitables not being accustomed to the ground, which our batsmen, of course, were perfectly familiar with; so runs got piled on in a way that raised our hopes pretty considerably, especially when Sidney Grant took Charley Bates's place—that worthy having in his second over skied a ball that was immediately caught, sending him out for five runs, two singles and a three, or two more than he had totalled in his last match.

It was a sight to see Sidney as he cut and drove the slow and fast bowlers of our opponents' team for four almost every over; whilst John Hardy backed him up ably by remaining, as he was instructed, strictly on the defensive, and blocking every ball that came at all near his wicket. Sidney was the run-getter; he had simply to run.

We had scored thirty-eight for the loss of

only one wicket, and the captain seemed to be well set and good to make the century—as he had done a month before in our match with the Smithwick Club—when a new bowler went on at the lower end of the ground, and "a change came over the spirit of our dream."

"I don't like the way that chap walks up to the wicket," said Tom Atkins to me. "I saw him taking Sidney's measure when he was serving as long stop, and if he doesn't play carefully, he'll bowl him out almost with his first ball."

"Not he," said I sanguinely. "He seems too confident."

"Ah well! we'll see," replied Tom.

That new bowler was something awful. He sent in the balls at such a pace that they came on the wicket like battering-rams, and their twist was so great that they would pitch about a mile off and appear to be wides, when all of a sudden they would spin in on a treacherous curve, right on to a fellow's leg stump. John Hardy stood them well enough, blocking away with a calm sense of duty, and never attempting to strike one. But poor Sidney lost his head in a very short time, and hitting out wildly at what he thought was a short ball, it rose right over the shoulder of his bat and carried off his bails in the neatest manner possible—two wickets for forty-one runs, as the captain had only managed to put on three runs since that fiend in human form had come on to bowl.

Of course there was a wild shout of victory from the Inimitables when our best bat was disposed of, and corresponding woe in our camp, which was sympathizingly shared in by all the Little Peddlingtons around, and in the midst of the excitement I went to the wicket to fill the lamented vacancy.

"Mind, Jack," said Sidney, who did not allow the sense of defeat to overcome his duty, "and be certain to play those balls well back. It was all through my stepping out to them that caused my collapse. Only be cautious and take things coolly, and you and Prester John will tire him out."

"Oh, yes," sneered Charley Bates, whose temper had not been improved by his getting out for five, when, in spite of his assurances of the superiority of our antagonists, he had looked forward to getting the highest score against them,—" Oh, yes. Tire him out! Why, the chap hasn't got into the use of his arm yet. He'll send Jack Limpet's stumps flying presently. But I shall laugh when Tom Atkins faces his balls! Our comic man won't have anything to joke about then, I'll warrant."

He was a nasty fellow that Charley Bates! I don't know anything more ungenerous than to try and dishearten a fellow just when he is going to the wicket, and knows what a responsibility he has resting on him! But, then, what can you expect from such a chap? I'm glad he got out for five. I wish he had been bowled for nix.

With these pleasant thoughts in my mind I walked leisurely up the ground from where I had been standing by the scoring tent watching the game, and with an inward sinking at my heart faced the "Slogger," as we had christened our opponents' terrible bowler.

For a couple of overs I got on very well. Acting on the captain's advice I stopped in my own ground, playing all the Slogger's balls carefully back, and by this means managed to score two good leg hits in the fourth over, that sent up six to my account, in addition to three singles, which I had put on by careful watchfulness at first.

Just then, however, Prester John made a hit for a wonder—a straight drive for five; and fired with emulation I let out at the next ball I received. Throwing all caution and the captain's commands to the winds, I did "let out with a vengeance," as Tom Atkins said on my return to the tent, for I "let in" the ball, which, coming in with a swish, snapped my leg-stump in two, sending the pieces flying sky high in the air!

Three wickets for fifty-seven runs, two for byes; so far, the scoring was not bad; but in a very short time Pelion was piled on Ossa in the history of our disasters. Prester John got run out through the absurd folly of Tom Atkins, who stopped actually in mid-wicket to laugh at some nonsense or other that had at that moment flashed across the vision of what he called his "mind;" and with his fall our chances sank rapidly to zero, wicket after wicket being taken without a run being scored, until the whole of us were out for a total still under sixty.

It was maddening! But what annoyed John Hardy even more than that ass Tom Atkins having run him out was that the captain had never given young James Black any opportunity of showing his batting skill, as, being persuaded by Charley Bates, who pooh-poohed the youngster's abilities *in toto*, he had only sent him in as "last-man," and Black hadn't, of course, the chance of playing a ball. Sidney, however, promised to right the matter in our second innings, should our opponents give us time to play one, and not occupy the wickets, as seemed very probable, for the two days over which the match could only extend: and with this promise Prester John and his protégé, young Jemmy Black, were fain to be content.

The three recruits we had engaged from amongst the visitors to join our scratch eleven had, up to the present, done nothing to warrant our captain's encomiums on their skill—at least in the batting line, which they had only essayed as yet; it remained to be proved whether they were worth anything in the field; if not, then our chances of receiving a hollow licking were uncommonly bright, as Charley Bates pointed out with his customary cheerful irony.

Well, after luncheon, when we entertained them in the most hospitable manner, as if we loved them instead of feeling sentiments the reverse of amicable towards them, the Inimitables went in for their first innings; and the way they set to work scoring from the moment they commenced to handle the bat, prognosticated that Charley Bates' evil surmise as to our defeat would be speedily realized.

I think I have already hinted that I somewhat prided myself on my bowling, being celebrated amongst the members of the Little Peddlington Cricket Club for sending in slows of such a judicious pitch that they generally got the man caught out who attempted to drive them, while, should he contemptuously block them, they had such an underhand twist that they would invariably run into the wickets, although they mightn't seem to have strength to go the distance?

From this speciality of mine I was looked upon as a tower of strength in the bowling line to the club; and, consequently, I and one of our visitor recruits, Tomkins by name, were intrusted with the ball at the first start.

Tomkins bowled swift with a pretty fair pitch, and I bowled slow, dead on to the wicket every time; but the two men of the Inimitables who began the batting on their side—men who have gained almost a European reputation in the handling of the willow, and I wouldn't like to hurt their feelings by mentioning their names now—seemed to play with us as they liked, hitting the ball to every part of the ground, and scoring threes and fours, and even sixes, in the most demoralizing manner possible. They hadn't been in a quarter of an hour when they passed our miserable total, amidst the cheers of their own party—in which the fickle Little Peddlingtonians now joined, and the blue looks of our men—and it appeared as if their scoring would, like Tennyson's brook, "go on for ever."

"We must put a stop to this," said Sidney,

when seventy went up on the scoring-board, "and change the bowling," which he did, by going on himself at my end and putting one of the other visitors, who was also supposed to be a dab with the ball, in the place of Tomkins.

For a time, this did a little good, as it stopped the rapidity of the scoring; but after an over or two, the batsmen, neither of whom had been yet displaced, began putting up the runs again, even quicker than they had done with us; and the hundred was passed almost within the hour from the time they started.

"By George, Limpet," said the captain, calling me to him out of the field, "you must go on again at the upper end, changing places with that chap. Try a full pitch, and we'll catch that long-legged beggar out; he's so confident now that he would hit at anything."

Going on again, as Sidney had directed, I tried a full-pitched ball after a short delivery or two, and the "long-legged beggar" skied it, amidst the breathless suspense of our team.

Unfortunately, however, no one was there

to catch it when it fell to the ground a long way beyond cover-point, and the Inimitables scored six for it—disgusting!

"That Atkins deserves to be expelled the club!" said the captain in a rage. "He can't put on a bit of steam when it's necessary to use his legs, although he could run Prester John out for a ball that wasn't worth moving for. Play!" And the game went on again.

Giving my opponent another brace of short balls to take him off his guard, I watched my opportunity again and treated him again to a full one, which he skied, as before, to the same point.

This time, however, he did not escape scatheless. Young Black, whom I had strangely missed from his position at long-stop since I commenced to bowl the over, stepped out from beneath the shadow of the trees, where he had concealed himself in the meantime, and amidst the ringing plaudits, not only of our lot but of the spectators as well—who turned round in our favour at the first breath of success—caught the ball with the utmost *sang froid*, sending it a moment afterwards spinning in the air triumphantly, in the true cricketonian manner, as an acknowledgment of the feat and accompanying cheers.

It wasn't much to brag of, getting out the long-limbed one, as it was only one wicket for one hundred and seventeen runs; but when the second man went shortly after without increasing the score, our hopes began to rise. They were hopes based on sand, however. The two new-comers began making runs just like their predecessors, and completely mastered the bowling.

Every member of the club had now been tried with the ball, besides the three visitors, who certainly bowled fairly well, but nothing hysterically brilliant. Even Charley Bates had a turn, although I don't believe he had ever hit the wicket in his life; and on his surrendering the ball, after presenting our opponents with three wides and any number of byes, our captain was at his wits' end. He didn't know who he could set on to bowl.

"**Try** young Black," suggested Hardy at this juncture, when we were having a short interval of rest from our exhilarating game of leather-hunting, which had now been going on for two hours and more.

"Young Black, indeed!" repeated Charley Bates with intense scorn.

"Well," said Prester John, "he can't possibly do worse than you."

And the remark was so painfully true that even Charley could not but see the point of it, and he said no more.

On being called, Jemmy Black came up with a broad grin on his face, which looked exactly like one of those public-house signs you sometimes see in country villages, of "The Rising Sun," or "The Sun in Splendour." He was otherwise a dapper little fellow, although scarcely five feet in height, and strongly built, his legs and arms being very muscular.

He endeavoured to receive with proper gravity and dignity the ball from Sidney, who gave him a few words of appropriate advice, but he failed utterly in the attempt. That grin would not leave his face: it was as much a part of his physiognomy as his nose, I believe!

Little chap as he was, however, his advent

produced a change at once. His first three overs were maidens, balls that were dead on to the wicket, and so true and ticklish that the Inimitable champions did not dare to play them. In the next, bang went one of the two stickers' leg stump at young Black's first ball; with the second he caught and bowled the fresh man who came in, before he scored at all—four wickets for a hundred and fifty runs, not one of which had been put on since he came on to bowl. Things began to look up, or, at all events, did not appear in so sombre a light as they had done previously.

"Bravo, Black!" resounded from every part of the field; but the little fellow took no notice of the applause, beyond grinning more widely than ever, "his mouth stretching from ear to ear," as Charley Bates said, green with envy and jealousy of the other's performance.

The new bowler seemed to demoralize the batsmen even as they had previously demoralized us, for I had a bit of luck a little further on, taking one wicket by a low-pitched ball, and getting another man out with a catch; and then Black, as if he had been only playing with the Inimitables hitherto, braced himself up to the struggle, and began laying the stumps low right and left.

It was a wonder that such a small chap could send in the balls at the terrific speed he did, balls that set leg-guards and pads at defiance, and splintered one of the batsmen's spring-handled bats as if it had been matchwood; but he did it.

His last over in that first innings of the Inimitables, however, was the crowning point in his victorious career. With four consecutive balls he took the four last wickets of our opponents, and sent them off the ground without putting up a run—the whole eleven being out for one hundred and fifty-six runs —or not quite the century beyond us; and the principal feature of Black's triumph was, that from the moment he handled the leather, the Inimitables only scored six to the good, but one run of which was off his bowling.

I should like you to beat that analysis, if you can!

With the disposal of our antagonists so

easily at the end, we began our second innings with more sanguine expectations than could have been imagined from our previous prostration.

"Black had better go in as first man along with you, Hardy, and see what he can do," our captain said.

The two accordingly went to the wickets at the beginning of the innings; and there they remained without giving a single chance until the conclusion of the day's play, when the stumps were drawn at seven o'clock in the evening.

Young Black had scored by that time no less than eighty off his own bat, and Hardy forty-one, after being in to their own cheek exactly as long as the Inimitables' whole innings lasted. It was glorious, one hundred and eighteen without the loss of a wicket, and the bowling and fielding must have been good, as there were only seven extras all that long while our men had been in. Why, that placed us thirty-one runs to the good at the close of the first day's play. Who would have thought it?

The next morning play began as punctually as on the first day, and the crowd to witness the match was even greater than before, many coming now who had stayed away previously, expecting our wholesale defeat in one innings; and "young Ebony," as Black was called affectionately, and Prester John resumed their places at the wickets amidst the tremendous cheering from the whole of the hamlet and twenty miles round.

The bowlers of the Inimitables were on their metal now if they never were; but they bowled, and changed their bowling, in vain, for young Jemmy Black continued his brilliant hitting without any cessation, while Prester John remained on the defensive, except some very safe ball tempted him, until our score turned the two hundred in our second innings.

Prester John here retired by reason of his placing a ball in short-slip's hands; but on our captain taking his place and facing Black, the run-getting went steadily on until we were considerably a hundred over our antagonists. Young Black had not given a chance, save one close shave of a run out, when he got clean bowled for one hundred and fifty-one. Fancy that; and off such first-class bowling, too!

It was as much as Hardy and I could do to prevent him being torn in pieces by the excited spectators, who rushed in *en masse* when he abandoned the wicket he had defended so well, his face all the time expanding into one huge grin, which appeared to convert it into all mouth and nothing else.

Sidney and I, and one or two others, scored well, although nothing like what our two champion stickers had done; and the whole of our second innings terminated for two hundred and eighty-eight runs, thus leaving the Inimitables no less than a hundred and ninety-one to get to tie us, and one more to win. I fancy that was something like a feather in the cap of the Little Peddlington Cricket Club, although it was all owing to young Jemmy Black, whose bowling, when the Inimitables went in to make their final effort, was on a par with his magnificent batting. We had finished our second innings just before lunch time; so immediately after that meal the great traveling team, who were going to do such wonders when they came to annihilate the Little Peddlingtonians—I can't help crowing a little now it is all over—went to the wickets to finish the match, or spin it out, if they could, so that it might end in a draw.

Young Black was all there, however, and so was I, too, for, whether by his example or what, I know not, I never bowled so well before or since in my life. Really, between us two, and the efficient assistance of our fieldsmen, who seemed also spurred up to extra exertions, even Charley Bates and Tom Atkins distinguishing themselves for their quickness of eye and fleetness of foot, the Piccadilly Inimitables got all put out long before time was called, for the inglorious total of our own first innings—fifty-nine. Hurrah!

We had conquered by a hundred and thirty-two runs, and licked the most celebrated amateur club in England. It would be a vain task to try and recount our delighted surprise, so I'll leave it alone. Thenceforward the rest of the chronicles of the Little Peddlington Cricket Club are they not written in gold? At all events, I know this, that we never forgot what happened to us in that ever-memorable match, with only "Our Scratch Eleven."

www.ingramcontent.com/pod-product-compliance
Lightning Source LLC
Chambersburg PA
CBHW030316170426
43202CB00009B/1019